Applications of Genetics

Jennifer Gregory

Series editor
Fred Webber

CAMBRIDGE
UNIVERSITY PRESS

Published by the Press Syndicate of the University of Cambridge
The Pitt Building, Trumpington Street, Cambridge CB2 1RP
40 West 20th Street, New York, NY 10011-4211, USA
10 Stamford Road, Oakleigh, Melbourne 3166, Australia

© University of Cambridge Local Examinations Syndicate 1995

First published 1995

Printed in Great Britain at the University Press, Cambridge

A catalogue record for this book is available from the British Library

ISBN 0 521 48503 7 paperback

Designed and produced by Gecko Ltd, Bicester, Oxon

This book is one of a series produced to support
individual modules within the Cambridge Modular
Sciences scheme. Teachers should note that written
examinations will be set on the content of each module as
defined in the syllabus. This book is the author's
interpretation of the module.

Cover: Dendrobium diorcs × am flora:
varieties of this genus are commercially propagated for the cut-flower
market using tissue culture.

Acknowledgements

Photographs

1.4a, John Daniels/Ardea; 1.4b, Jean Paul
Ferrero/Ardea; 1.6, Dr Jeremy Burgess/
Science Photo Library; 1.8, 5.3, Biophoto
Associates; 2.3, PBI (Cambridge) Ltd; 2.4,
Peter Rossdale; 2.5, 4.7, Hank Morgan/
Science Photo Library; 2.6, Pete Addis/
Environmental Picture Library; 2.7, 3.4, 3.6,
4.9, Nigel Cattlin/Holt Studios; 3.1, 3.2,
Connecticut Agricultural Experiment Station;
3.3, Royal Botanic Gardens, Kew; 3.5,
Philippe Plailly/Science Photo Library; 3.9,
Prof Stanley Cohen/Science Photo Library;
3.11, Dr L Caro/Science Photo Library; 4.12,
Nature; 5.2, CNRI/Science Photo Library; 5.8,
Bourne Hall/ISC Presentations; 5.10, 5.14,
Peter Menzel/ Science Photo Library; 5.15, J C
Revy/ Science Photo Library; 5.17, DRCT/
Custom Medical Stock/Science Photo Library.

Diagrams

1.7, after fig 5.1 *Elementary Genetics* Wilma
George, 1965, 2nd ed. Macmillan; 3.8, after
*Dalton's Introduction to Practical Animal
Breeding* Willis, 1991, Blackwell Scientific
Publications; 3.13, data replotted from
Metcalf, *Scientific American*, October 1952;
3.14, modified from *Ecological impact of
pesticide use in developing countries* van der
Valk & Koeman, 1988, Ministry of Housing,
Physical Planning and Environment, Hague,
Netherlands, and World Wide Fund for
Nature, UK, Data Support for Education
Service, July 1990; 5.5, from *Applied
Genetics* Hayward, 1990, Macmillan Science
16–19 Project, Macmillan; 5.9, after
Genetics and Evolution M. Carter, 1993,
Hodder and Stoughton.

Tables

3.1, data from *Handbook of Genetics*
Whitten *et al.*, vol. 3, 1975, cd. R. C. King,
Plenum Press, New York; 4.2, data modified
from Cory *et al.* reprinted with permission
from *Nature* **370**, 138–40, copyright (1994)
Macmillan Magazines Ltd.

Contents

Introduction

The applications of genetics cover a very wide field, only certain parts of which can be covered within the confines of this book. The book's primary role is to support *Applications of Genetics* in the University of Cambridge Local Examinations Syndicate (UCLES) A level syllabuses, but it can also be used to cover similar material in other syllabuses. The aim is to develop an understanding of:

- the causes of variation;
- the principles and uses of selective breeding;
- the importance of genetic diversity;
- the ways in which organisms can be modified by genetic engineering and the benefits, hazards and ethical implications of such changes;
- some aspects of human genetics and an appreciation of their medical, ethical and social implications.

The material in this book assumes that the reader has knowledge of the structure and replication of DNA, and its role in protein synthesis; a basic understanding of genes, alleles, monohybrid and dihybrid crosses; and the role of natural selection in evolution.

The book is divided into five chapters, each concerned with one of the five aims given above. The first chapter considers the variation of living organisms and how that variation is described and measured. There is a genetic and an environmental component to variation, both of which are considered. Understanding the genetic component of variation will involve you in more complex inheritance patterns than the classic Mendelian crosses that you will have met already. If you are not confident about the genetics of such crosses, you can read about them in chapter 5 of *Central Concepts in Biology* in this series. This chapter finishes with the use of one of the standard statistical methods for testing the significance of the results of genetic crosses.

When an applied geneticist understands how variation is inherited, that knowledge can be put to use in the selective breeding of organisms. In selective breeding, desirable characteristics are selected for. Chapter 2 looks at the principles of selective breeding and gives examples of its use in both plants and animals. Although the process is essentially the same in both plants and animals, the complexities of reproduction in mammals requires the use of all the techniques of reproductive technology: artificial insemination, in vitro fertilisation and the cloning and transplantation of embryos.

Genetic diversity is reduced by inbreeding populations and by selection, held stable by cloning organisms, or increased by mutation. Chapter 3 looks at these aspects of diversity, including the importance of maintaining diversity in gene banks. The examples of mutation and selection involve resistance of animals and plants to disease, of bacteria to antibiotics and of insects to pesticides.

Selective breeding gradually modifies the whole genetic complement of an organism, but in genetic engineering one gene, or a few genes, are transferred from one organism to another. In chapter 4 you will meet the techniques of genetic engineering, some examples of its use, its benefits and possible hazards. Before starting this chapter you will need to be familiar with the structure of DNA and RNA. You can read about them in chapter 4 of *Central Concepts in Biology*.

The last chapter describes three human genetic disorders, genetic screening and gene therapy. The use of genetic fingerprinting to demonstrate human variation and the significance of variation in transplant surgery are also considered.

This area of science is developing very rapidly. The announcements of newly identified genes or of newly genetically engineered organisms come almost daily. Hence, some of the information given in the book will become out of date, and the examples given will need to be replaced by others, perhaps with different ethical implications. You should, therefore, be prepared to keep up-to-date, by reading relevant articles in newspapers and in journals such as *New Scientist*. Discuss with your friends the ethical implications of new discoveries and procedures.

Variation

Living organisms vary. The applied geneticist must be able to recognise the extent of this variation and to distinguish inherited variation from that caused by the environment. Only when the geneticist has that information can it be applied to such fields as selective breeding, genetic engineering and human genetics. The first step, then, is to describe and measure the extent of variation.

Discontinuous and continuous variation

The total appearance of an organism is called its **phenotype**. Phenotypic differences between you and your friends include **qualitative** differences, such as different blood groups, and **quantitative** differences such as height and mass.

Qualitative characteristics fall into clearly distinguishable categories, with no intermediates. You are either male or female, and have also only one of four possible ABO blood groups: A, B, AB or O. This is **discontinuous variation**. In contrast, the quantitative differences between individual heights or masses may be small and difficult to distinguish. When the height of a large number of people is measured, there are no distinguishable height classes. Instead there is a range of heights between two extremes *(figure 1.1)*. This is **continuous variation**.

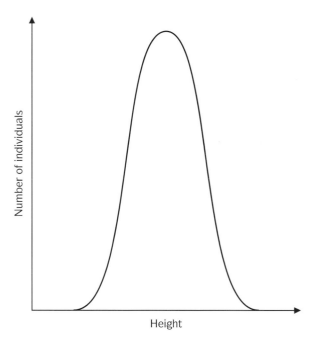

● *Figure 1.1* Distribution curve showing continuous variation.

Variance

The variation shown by a quantitative character can be given by the **variance**, which is a measure of how much spread there is about the **mean** (average) value for the character. *Figure 1.2* shows two distribution curves with different variances. Different variances in phenotype result from differences in both an organism's **genotype** (an organism's genetic make-up) and the effects of its environment, as will be seen later.

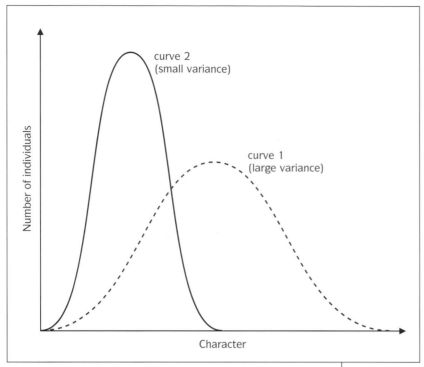

● *Figure 1.2* Distribution curves with different variances; curve 1 shows a large variance and curve 2 a small variance.

A worked example showing how to calculate the mean and variance of a quantitative character is shown in *box 1A*.

The genetic basis of discontinuous and continuous variation

Both qualitative and quantitative differences in phenotype may be inherited via genes. Both may involve several different gene loci. However, there are important differences between them.

In discontinuous (qualitative) variation:

- different alleles at a single gene locus have large effects;
- different gene loci have quite different effects on the character.

In continuous (quantitative) variation:

- different alleles at a gene locus have small effects;
- different gene loci have the same, often additive, effect on the character;
- a large number of loci may have a combined effect on a particular phenotypic character. These are known as **polygenes**.

Box 1A

A sample of maize cobs, from a variety known as Tom Thumb, was taken and the cobs measured to the nearest centimetre. The number of cobs in each centimetre length category was counted:

	Cob length/cm			
	5	*6*	*7*	*8*
Number of cobs in each length category (n)	4	21	24	8

The mean cob length $(\bar{x})$ = sum (Σ) of all the cob lengths (x)/number (n) of cobs, or = $\Sigma x/n$

$$\bar{x} = (5 \times 4)+(6 \times 21)+(7 \times 24)+(8 \times 8)/57 \, \text{cm}$$
$$= 378/57 \, \text{cm}$$
$$= 6.63 \, \text{cm}$$

$$\text{Variance} = \frac{\Sigma n(x - \bar{x})^2}{\Sigma n - 1}$$

$\Sigma n = 57$
$\Sigma(x - \bar{x})^2 = 37.44 \, \text{cm}^2$

$$\text{Variance} = \frac{37.44}{57 - 1} = 0.67 \, \text{cm}^2$$

Number of cobs in each length category (n)	*x/cm*	$(x - \bar{x})/cm$	$(x - \bar{x})^2/cm^2$	$n(x - \bar{x})^2/cm^2$
4	5	−1.63	2.66	10.64
21	6	−0.63	0.40	8.40
24	7	0.37	0.14	3.36
8	8	1.37	1.88	15.04

Discontinuous variation

Different alleles at a single locus

If possible, look again at chapter 5 of *Central Concepts in Biology* in this series. You will find there a number of examples of the inheritance of discontinuous variation showing the large effects of the different alleles of a single gene. The inheritance of the β-polypeptide gene of haemoglobin and of the gene responsible for red, pink and white flower colour in snapdragons (*Antirrhinum*) both show the effect of two **codominant** alleles, that is alleles which both have an effect on the phenotype in a heterozygote. In snapdragons, the two alleles of this flower colour gene are C^R which gives red flowers, and C^W which gives white flowers. The phenotypes produced by each genotype are:

Genotype	Phenotype
$C^R C^R$	red flowers
$C^R C^W$	pink flowers
$C^W C^W$	white flowers

The inheritance of purple and green stem colour in tomato plants shows the inheritance of two alleles of a gene of which only one, the **dominant** allele, has an effect in the heterozygote. In a tomato plant which has one allele for purple stems and one allele for green stems, the stems are purple. The allele for green stems is said to be **recessive**.

Most genes have more than two alleles. The inheritance of the human ABO blood groups provides an example of this situation, known as **multiple alleles**. It also shows both dominance and codominance of the alleles concerned. The four blood groups, A, B, AB and O, are determined by three alleles of a single gene: I^A, I^B and I^o. I^A and I^B are codominant, whilst I^o is recessive to both I^A and I^B. The possible genotypes and phenotypes are:

Genotype	Phenotype (blood group)
$I^A I^A$	A
$I^A I^o$	A
$I^B I^B$	B
$I^B I^o$	B
$I^A I^B$	AB
$I^o I^o$	O

A woman with blood group A and a man with blood group B, both of whom were heterozygous at the ABO locus, could produce a child with any one of the ABO blood groups:

Parent's phenotypes	female with blood group A	male with blood group B
Parent's genotypes	$I^A I^o$	$I^B I^o$
Gametes	I^A or I^o	I^B or I^o

Offspring genotypes and phenotypes

		Gametes from woman	
		I^A	I^o
Gametes from man	I^B	$I^A I^B$ group AB	$I^B I^o$ group B
	I^o	$I^A I^o$ group A	$I^o I^o$ group O

Each time this couple have a child there is an equal (0.25%) probability that it will have any one of the blood groups A, B, AB or O.

Now look at an example of discontinuous variation that you will find useful when considering the genetic basis of resistance in chapter 3: the inheritance of resistance to warfarin in rats.

Warfarin was introduced as a rat poison in the 1950s. It interferes with vitamin K metabolism and so prevents blood clotting: the rats die from internal bleeding. By the end of the 1950s warfarin-resistant rats had been found in Scotland, and over the next 20 years they were found in other areas of the United Kingdom too.

Resistance is controlled at a single gene locus. In this case the gene (Rw, for resistance to warfarin) has two alleles:

Rw^R = the allele giving resistance to warfarin
Rw^S = the allele giving susceptibility to warfarin.

Three genotypes are possible, each giving a different phenotype as shown in *table 1.1*.

Genotype	Phenotype	
	resistance to warfarin	vitamin K requirement
Rw^SRw^S	susceptible	normal
Rw^RRw^S	resistant	slightly increased
Rw^RRw^R	resistant	high

● *Table 1.1*

SAQ 1.1

Draw a genetic diagram to show the offspring expected from crossing two rats heterozygous at this locus.

Different gene loci

In discontinuous variation, different gene loci have different effects on a phenotypic character. For example, in tomato plants, a number of genes code for different features of the plants' leaves. Among others, one gene codes for leaf shape, another for the presence or absence of hairs on the leaves and a third for the presence or absence of chlorophyll.

Genes at different loci may also interact to produce discontinuous variation, as in epistasis (page 7).

Continuous variation

Two of the typical effects of the inheritance of continuous variation, namely the small effects of the different alleles of one gene on a phenotypic character, and the additive effect of different genes on the same character, may be seen in a hypothetical example of the inheritance of an organism's height.

Suppose that the height of an organism is controlled by two, unlinked (that is, on different chromosomes) gene loci, **A/a** and **B/b**, and that the recessive alleles of both loci (**a** and **b**) each contribute x cm to the height of the organism, whereas the dominant alleles (**A** and **B**) each increase the height by $2x$ cm.

If the effect of each gene is additive, the homozygote recessive, **aabb**, therefore is potentially $4x$ cm tall and the homozygote dominant **AABB** is potentially $8x$ cm tall. The other genotypes will fall between these extremes.

Suppose now that the homozygotes, **aabb** and **AABB**, are interbred.

Parent's phenotypes	$4x$ cm tall	$8x$ cm tall
Parent's genotypes	aabb	AABB
Gametes	ab	AB
F_1 genotypes	AaBb	
F_1 phenotypes	all $6x$ cm tall	

Interbreeding the F_1 generation *(box 1B)* gives all possible genotypes amongst the 16 possibilities:

Gametes from one parent

	AB	Ab	aB	ab
AB	AABB $8x$ cm	AABb $7x$ cm	AaBB $7x$ cm	AaBb $6x$ cm
Ab	AABb $7x$ cm	AAbb $6x$ cm	AaBb $6x$ cm	Aabb $5x$ cm
aB	AaBB $7x$ cm	AaBb $6x$ cm	aaBB $6x$ cm	aaBb $5x$ cm
ab	AaBb $6x$ cm	Aabb $5x$ cm	aaBb $5x$ cm	aabb $4x$ cm

Gametes from the other parent

The number of offspring and their potential heights according to their genotypes are summarised in *figure 1.3*. These results fall approximately on a normal distribution curve.

These imaginary results come from assuming that two gene loci on different chromosomes contribute to the height of the organism. Think about what will happen to a quantitative character if more gene loci, each with an additive effect, are involved (**polygenes**). Suppose that all the genes affecting height are on different chromosomes: the number of discrete height classes increases as more genes are involved, and the difference between these classes gets less. Even if two or more of the loci are linked on the same chromosome (page 8), potentially reducing the number of classes of offspring and increasing the difference between them, crossing over in prophase I of meiosis (page 10) will restore the variation. The differences between different classes will be further smoothed out by environmental effects, as discussed in the next section.

Potential height from genotype	4x cm	5x cm	6x cm	7x cm	8x cm
Number of offspring with that genotype/16	1	4	6	4	1

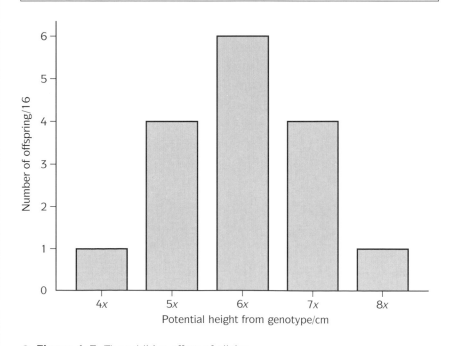

● *Figure 1.3* The additive effect of alleles.

Both genotype and environment contribute to phenotypic variance

In the imaginary example of continuous variation just given, the heights shown are those expected from the genotype alone. If you were able to take a number of individuals, all with the same genotypic contribution to height, it would be most unlikely that their height would be exactly the same when measured. Environmental effects may allow the full genetic potential height to be reached or may stunt it in some way.

One individual animal might have less food, or less nutritious food, than another with the same genetic contribution. A plant may be in a lower light intensity or in soil with fewer nutrients than another with the same genetic potential height. Other examples of the effect of environment include the development of dark tips to ears, nose, paws and tail in the Himalayan colouring of rabbits and in Siamese cats. This colouring is caused by an allele which allows the formation of the dark pigment only at low temperature. The extremities are the coldest parts of the animals, so the colour is produced there.

When the number of gene loci controlling a quantitative character is large, it is not possible to identify them and assess the individual effects of their various alleles.

In selective breeding (chapter 2), it is important to know how much of the phenotypic variation is genetic, and how much is environmental in origin. There is no point in selecting parents for a breeding programme on the basis of environmental variation!

The genetic and environmental contributions to phenotypic variation are written simply:

$$V_P = V_G + V_E$$

where V_P is the phenotypic variation, V_G is the genetic component, and V_E is the environmental component of the variation. The proportion of the phenotypic variation that is genetic is referred to as the **heritability** of the character. Successful selective breeding requires a high heritability.

In a classic experiment the American geneticists Ralph Emerson and Edward East crossed two varieties of maize which differed markedly in cob length. Both of the parental varieties (Black Mexican and Tom Thumb) were pure-bred lines. The cob lengths of the plants used as parents and the first and second generations of offspring resulting from the cross were measured to the nearest centimetre. The number of cobs in each length category was counted. The results are shown in *table 1.2*.

Both parental varieties were pure-bred and therefore homozygous at a large number of loci. The first generation of offspring were genetically different from the parents, but were genetically the same as one another. The phenotypic variation that we see within the two parental lines and within the first generation is, therefore, environmental.

The average variance of the two parental varieties and of the first generation of offspring provides a measure of the environmental variance (V_E).

The second generation of offspring shows a much wider range of variation in cob length. This is both genetic and environmental.

SAQ 1.2

a From *table 1.2*, calculate the variance in cob length (V_P) shown by the Black Mexican parental variety and by the first generation of offspring. The variance of the Tom Thumb parental variety has already been calculated in *box 1A*.

b Calculate the environmental variance, V_E.

c Calculate the phenotypic variance (V_P) of the second generation of offspring, and from this, and your answer to **b**, find the genetic component of the variance (V_G).

Interactions at one locus and between loci

The interactions between alleles at the same locus, of codominant alleles (as in flower colour in *Antirrhinum*), dominant and recessive alleles (as in tomato plant stem colour) and multiple alleles (as in the inheritance of ABO blood groups in humans), have already been discussed on page 3.

However, there are cases where different loci interact to affect one phenotypic character. When one gene locus (the **epistatic** gene) affects or inhibits the effect of another locus (the **hypostatic** gene), this is known as **epistasis**.

Epistasis

In the inheritance of feather colour in chickens there is an interaction between two gene loci, **I/i** and **C/c**. Individuals carrying the dominant allele, **I**, have white feathers even if they also carry the dominant allele, **C**, for coloured feathers. Birds that are homozygous recessive, **cc**, are also white. This is an example of **dominant epistasis**.

									Cob length/cm								
	5	6	7	8	9	10	11	12	13	14	15	16	17	18	19	20	21
Black Mexican parents								3	11	12	14	26	15	10	7	2	
Tom Thumb parents	4	21	24	8													
Offspring 1					1	12	12	14	17	9	4						
Offspring 2			1	10	19	26	47	73	68	68	39	25	15	9	1		

● *Table 1.2* Variation in cob length of two parental varieties of maize and of the first and second generations of a cross between them

● **Figure 1.4**

a White Leghorn and **b** white Wyandotte chickens.

SAQ 1.3

List the genotypes that will result in coloured feathers.

White Leghorn chickens *(figure 1.4)* have the genotype **IICC**, whilst white Wyandotte chickens have the genotype **iicc**. A white Leghorn is crossed with a white Wyandotte.

Parent's phenotypes	white	white
Parent's genotypes	IICC	iicc
Gametes	(IC)	(ic)
F_1 *genotypes*	all IiCc	
F_1 *phenotypes*	white	

Now the F_1 offspring are interbred to give an F_2 generation.

Parent's genotypes	IiCc	IiCc
Gametes	(IC) or (Ic) or (iC) or (ic)	(IC) or (Ic) or (iC) or (ic)

Gametes from one parent

	(IC)	(Ic)	(iC)	(ic)
(IC)	IICC white	IICc white	IiCC white	IiCc white
(Ic)	IICc white	IIcc white	IiCc white	Iicc white
(iC)	IiCC white	IiCc white	iiCC coloured	iiCc coloured
(ic)	IiCc white	Iicc white	iiCc coloured	iicc white

Gametes from the other parent

The usual Mendelian 9:3:3:1 ratio expected in the F_2 generation has been modified by epistasis to $(9+3+1):3 = 13$ white : 3 coloured.

A different type of epistasis, **recessive epistasis**, is shown by the inheritance of flower colour in *Salvia*. A pure-breeding, pink-flowered variety of *Salvia* was crossed with a pure-breeding, white-flowered variety. The F_1 generation had purple flowers. Interbreeding the F_1 to give an F_2 generation resulted in purple, pink and white-flowered plants, in a ratio of 9:3:4. Two loci on different chromosomes, **A/a** and **B/b**, are involved:

Genotype	Flower colour
A-B-	purple
A-bb	pink
aaB-	white
aabb	white

(- indicates that either allele of the gene may be present)

The homozygous recessive **aa** is epistatic to the **B/b** locus (the hypostatic gene). Neither the dominant allele, **B**, for purple flower colour, nor the recessive allele, **b**, for pink flower colour can be expressed in the absence of a dominant **A** allele.

SAQ 1.4

Draw a genetic diagram of the *Salvia* cross described above to show the 9:3:4 ratio in the F_2 generation.

A different modification of the F_2 dihybrid ratio involves **complementary genes**, where two genes act sequentially in a metabolic pathway. Only if a dominant allele of the first gene to act is present will a suitable substrate be formed to be further acted upon by a dominant allele of the second locus. For example, a cross between two pure-breeding varieties of white-flowered sweet pea gave offspring which all had purple flowers. Interbreeding these gave plants with purple or with white flowers in a 9:7 ratio = $9:(3+3+1)$. Two gene loci, **A/a** and **B/b**, on different chromosomes, are involved, and pigment production depends on their combined action. The dominant alleles, **A** and **B**, each code for an enzyme in the metabolic pathway of pigment production (*figure 1.5*). The recessive alleles do not code for functioning enzymes. Purple pigment can be produced only when both dominant alleles are present in the genotype.

SAQ 1.5

a State the genotypes of the two pure-breeding varieties of white-flowered sweet pea used in the cross above.

b Draw a genetic diagram of the cross to show the 9:7 ratio of the F_2 generation.

Epistasis is not inherited. It results from the interaction of the gene loci of a particular genotype. Look back to the section on continuous variation. The different alleles had an additive effect on height. If we were to introduce epistasis as well as dominance, the number of possible phenotypes would be much reduced. Dominance and epistasis reduce phenotypic variation.

Linkage

The number of phenotypic classes resulting from a cross is also reduced by the phenomenon known as linkage.

When two or more gene loci are on the same chromosome, they do not assort independently in meiosis as they would if they were on different chromosomes. The loci are said to be **linked**.

Drosophila normally has a striped body, and antennae ending in a much branched spike (*figure 1.6*). The gene for body colour and the gene for antennal shape are close together on the same chromosome (chromosome 3) and so are linked.

A black body, with no stripes, results from a recessive allele called **ebony**. A recessive allele for antennal shape, **aristopedia**, gives an antenna looking

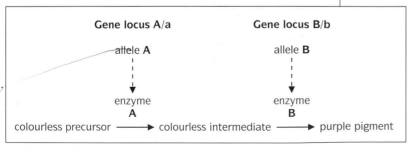

● *Figure 1.5* Pigment production pathway of flower colour in sweet pea.

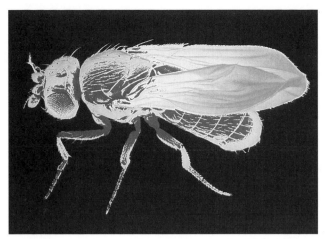

● *Figure 1.6* *Drosophila melanogaster* (× 20).

rather like a *Drosophila leg*, with two claws on the end (*figure 1.7*). A homozygous fly with a striped body and normal antennae was crossed with a homozygous ebony-bodied fly with aristopedia antennae. All the offspring had striped bodies and normal antennae. The male F_1 flies were then crossed with the parental type homozygous for ebony body and aristopedia antennae. This kind of cross, between the F_1 and the double recessive parental type, is known as a **test cross** and allows us to work out the genotype of the F_1. In this case the test cross produced the two original parental types in equal numbers in the offspring. This can be explained by the diagram on the right.

Body colour gene: E = allele for striped body
                       e = allele for ebony body
Antenna gene: A = allele for normal
                            antennae
                          a = allele for aristopedia
                            antennae

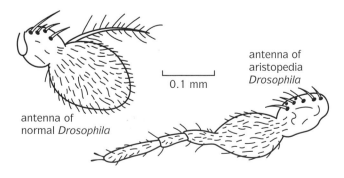

antenna of aristopedia *Drosophila*

0.1 mm

antenna of normal *Drosophila*

● *Figure 1.7* Normal and aristopedia *Drosophila* antennae.

To help you keep track of linked alleles in a genetic diagram, you should bracket each linkage group within a genotype. In this case the genotype of the striped body fly with normal antennae is written (EA)(EA) and not **EEAA**. (The latter would indicate that the genes were not on the same chromosome.)

Parent's phenotypes	striped body normal antennae	ebony body aristopedia antennae
Parent's genotypes	(EA)(EA)	(ea)(ea)
Gametes	EA	ea
F_1 genotype	all (EA)(ea)	
F_1 phenotype	striped body normal antennae	

The male F_1 offspring are test crossed:

	F_1 male	female
Parent's phenotypes	striped body normal antennae	ebony body aristopedia antennae
Parent's genotypes	(EA)(ea)	(ea)(ea)
Gametes	EA or ea	ea

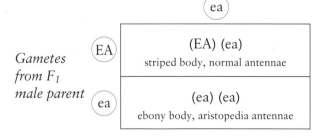

Gametes from female parent

Gametes from F_1 male parent	ea
EA	(EA) (ea) striped body, normal antennae
ea	(ea) (ea) ebony body, aristopedia antennae

The test cross gives a 1:1 ratio of the two original parental types and not the 1:1:1:1 ratio expected from a dihybrid test cross. (If you are uncertain about the 1:1:1:1 ratio, repeat the cross above but assume that the genes are **not** linked. This should result in 1EeAa:1Eeaa:1eeAa:1eeaa.)

The dihybrid cross has behaved as a monohybrid cross. The alleles that go into the cross together remain together.

The genes of any organism fall into a number of linkage groups equal to the number of pairs of homologous chromosomes. Total linkage is very rare. Almost always, linkage groups are broken by crossing over during meiosis. In the example above, a male *Drosophila* from the F₁ generation was test crossed to show the effect of linkage because, unusually, there is no crossing over in chromosomes of male *Drosophila*.

Crossing over

During prophase I of meiosis a pair of homologous chromosomes (a bivalent) can be seen to be joined by **chiasmata** *(figure 1.8)*. The chromatids of a bivalent may break and reconnect to another chromatid. This results in an exchange of gene loci between a maternal and paternal chromatid.

Let us return to the *Drosophila* cross given above, and test cross a female from the F₁ generation. *Figure 1.9* will help you follow what happens in the cross.

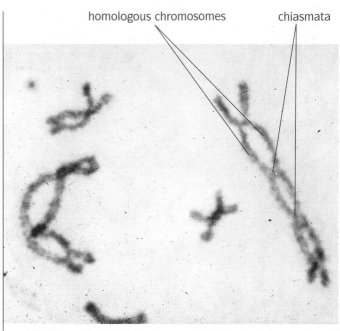

● *Figure 1.8* Photomicrograph of bivalents in prophase I of meiosis, showing chiasmata. A chiasma shows that crossing over has occurred between two chromatids.

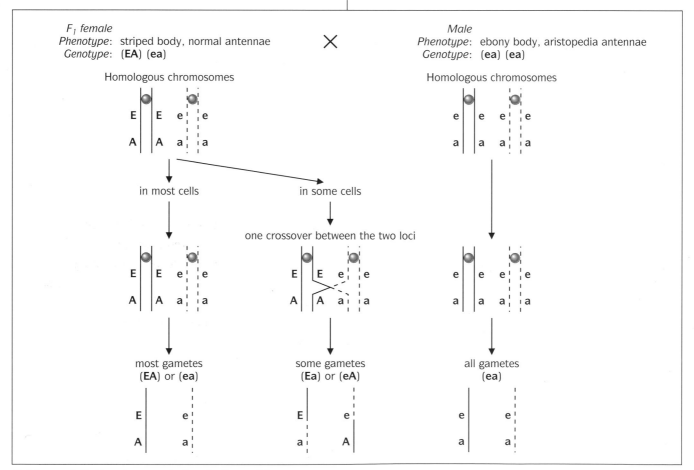

● *Figure 1.9* Crossing over in female *Drosophila*.

	F₁ female	male
Parent's phenotypes	striped body normal antennae	ebony body aristopedia antennae
Parent's genotypes	(EA)(ea)	(ea)(ea)
Gametes	large numbers of Ⓔ or ⓔ small numbers of Ⓔ or ⓔ from crossing over	ⓔ

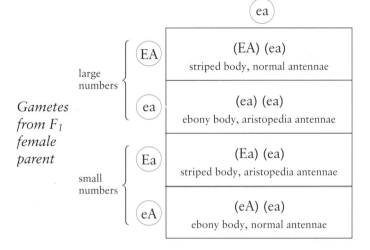

Gametes from male parent

ⓔ**a**

Gametes from F₁ female parent	large numbers	Ⓔ**A**	(EA) (ea) striped body, normal antennae
		ⓔ**a**	(ea) (ea) ebony body, aristopedia antennae
	small numbers	Ⓔ**a**	(Ea) (ea) striped body, aristopedia antennae
		ⓔ**A**	(eA) (ea) ebony body, normal antennae

Large numbers of the parental types of flies are produced. As you can see they are in a 1:1 ratio. Smaller numbers of **recombinant** flies are produced. These result from crossing over and 'recombine' the characteristics of the original parents into some flies that have a striped body with aristopedia antennae, and others that have an ebony body with normal antennae. The two recombinant classes themselves are in a 1:1 ratio.

In this particular cross we would typically find:

striped body, normal antennae	44%	} parental classes
ebony body, aristopedia antennae	44%	
striped body, aristopedia antennae	6%	} recombinant classes
ebony body, normal antennae	6%	

The **cross over value** is the percentage of offspring that belong to the recombinant classes. In this case it is 6% + 6% = 12%. This is a measure of the distance apart of the two gene loci on their chromosome. The smaller the cross over value, the closer the loci are together. The chance of a cross over occurring between two loci is directly related to their distance apart.

SAQ 1.6

Pure-breeding *Drosophila* with straight wings and grey bodies were crossed with pure-breeding curled-winged, ebony-bodied flies. The F₁ were all straight winged and grey bodied.

Female flies from the F₁ were then test crossed with curled-winged, ebony-bodied males, giving the following results:

straight wing, grey body	113
straight wing, ebony body	30
curled wing, grey body	29
curled wing, ebony body	115

a State the ratio of phenotypes expected in a dihybrid test cross such as this.

b Explain the discrepancy between the expected result and the results given.

c Calculate the cross over value.

d Is the curled wing locus closer to the ebony locus than is the aristopedia locus (see previous text)? Explain your answer.

The χ^2 (chi-squared) test

The ratios of phenotypes in a genetic cross represent probabilities. In a cross between a pink-flowered snapdragon, $C^R C^W$, and a white-flowered snapdragon, $C^W C^W$, there is an equal probability of a C^R gamete or a C^W gamete from the pink-flowered parent fusing with a C^W gamete from the white-flowered parent. We expect to see a 1:1 ratio of pink- and white-flowered offspring.

Suppose that among 100 offspring we find 52 pink-flowered plants and 48 white-flowered plants. We accept that such a small difference between the observed and expected results has occurred by chance. There is no reason to suppose that the original prediction of a 1:1 ratio was wrong.

But the larger the difference between the observed and expected results, the greater the likelihood that the original prediction was wrong. Suppose that the difference is so large that it would be expected to occur **by chance** in fewer than 1 in 20 experiments (a probability of 0.05). This is said to **differ significantly** from expectation and means that the original prediction cannot be upheld.

Conversely, if the difference between observed and expected results could occur **by chance** in **more** than 1 in 20 experiments, the results do not differ significantly from expectation, and the original prediction is supported.

The χ^2 test is a way of estimating the probability that differences between observed and expected results are due to chance.

The formula is:

$$\chi^2 = \sum \frac{\left(\begin{array}{c} \text{observed} \\ \text{number} \end{array} - \begin{array}{c} \text{expected} \\ \text{number} \end{array}\right)^2}{\text{expected number}}$$

- Differences are squared, making all numbers positive. If the differences were simply added together some differences would be larger than expected, giving a positive number and others smaller, giving a negative number. These might cancel out if added in this form.
- Dividing each (difference)^2 by the expected value is a way of allowing for the number of results.

We will now use the test on the data from **SAQ 1.6**. These were from a dihybrid test cross, so we expect the phenotypes of the offspring to be in a 1:1:1:1 ratio. The total number of offspring is 287.

Phenotypes of flies	straight wings, grey bodies	straight wings, ebony bodies	curled wings, grey bodies	curled wings, ebony bodies
Observed number (O)	113	30	29	115
Expected ratio	1 :	1 :	1 :	1
Expected number (E)	71.75	71.75	71.75	71.75
O − E	+41.25	−41.75	−42.75	+43.25
(O − E)^2	1701.6	1743.1	1827.6	1870.6
(O − E)^2/E	23.72	24.29	25.47	26.07

$\Sigma(O - E)^2/E = 99.55$

$\chi^2 = 99.55$

Degrees of freedom	Probability greater than			
	0.1	*0.05*	*0.01*	*0.001*
1	2.71	3.84	6.64	10.83
2	4.60	5.99	9.21	13.82
3	6.25	7.82	11.34	16.27
4	7.78	9.49	13.28	18.46

● **Table 1.3** Table of χ^2 values

Look now at *table 1.3*. This shows part of a table of χ^2 values and shows probabilities for different **degrees of freedom**. The degrees of freedom take account of the number of comparisons made. It is calculated as the (number of classes of data − 1). Here we have four classes of data, so the degrees of freedom = (4 − 1) = 3.

The table shows that the probability of $\chi^2 = 99.55$ is <0.001. (The value is so large that it is well off the right-hand side of the table.) We would not expect this difference from expectation to occur by chance in even 1 in 1000 experiments. The expected 1:1:1:1 ratio assumed independent assortment. This assumption now has to be rejected for these data, and another explanation looked for, that is linkage.

SAQ 1.7

Pure-breeding *Drosophila* with red eyes and normal bristles were crossed with pure-breeding flies with claret eyes and spineless (blunt) bristles. The F_1 flies all had red eyes and normal bristles.

Female flies from the F_1 were then test crossed with claret-eyed males with spineless bristles, giving the following results:

red-eyed flies with normal bristles	53
red-eyed flies with spineless bristles	34
claret-eyed flies with normal bristles	37
claret-eyed flies with spineless bristles	56

a Use the x^2 test and *table 1.3* to find the probability of the results of the test cross departing significantly from the expected ratio.

b What deduction can be made from the calculated x^2?

SUMMARY

Discontinuous variation of the phenotype is qualitative. Individuals fall into clearly distinguishable categories. Continuous variation, where the character shows a range between two extremes, is quantitative.

Variance measures how much spread there is about the mean for a quantitative character.

In discontinuous variation, the different alleles at a gene locus have large effects on the phenotype, and different gene loci have different effects.

In continuous variation, different alleles at a locus have small effects, and different gene loci have the same, often additive, effects on the phenotype. The character may be controlled by many gene loci (polygenes).

Both genotype and environment contribute to phenotypic variance.

When, in a heterozygote, only one allele has its effect on the phenotype of a heterozygote, it is said to be dominant. The allele which has no effect is recessive. When both alleles contribute to the phenotype they are said to be codominant.

Interaction between gene loci alters the expected phenotypic ratios in dihybrid crosses. One gene locus may inhibit the effect of another (epistasis), or the activity of one locus may depend on the activity of another (complementary genes).

When two or more gene loci are on the same chromosome, they do not assort independently in meiosis. The loci are said to be linked.

During prophase I of meiosis, the chromatids of a bivalent may break and reconnect. This may result in an exchange of gene loci between a maternal and a paternal chromatid, in a process called crossing over. Crossing over separates linked loci. Linkage alters the expected phenotypic ratios in dihybrid crosses.

The x^2 (chi-squared) test is a way of estimating the probability that differences between observed and expected results are due to chance.

Questions

1 **a** Using suitable examples from named species, explain what is meant by *discontinuous variation* and *continuous variation*.

b Explain what is meant by *variance*.

2 **a** Describe how the expression of alleles influences the phenotype.

b Discuss the effect the environment has on the phenotype.

3 **a** Describe how genetic variation may result from interactions at one locus and between loci.

b Suggest how you might assess the relative contributions of the genotype and the environment to the phenotype of an organism.

4 **a** With reference to suitable examples, explain the meaning of the terms *linkage* and *crossing over*.

b Explain the effect of linkage and crossing over on the phenotypic ratios from dihybrid crosses.

Selective breeding

The desirable characteristics of organisms may be selected for by selective breeding. In principle, the process of selective breeding is the same for all organisms, and may be compared with evolution by natural selection but with humans as the selective agent. However, the differences between plant and animal reproduction mean that different techniques are involved in their selective breeding, as will be seen below.

Selective breeding

When humans apply selection pressures to populations, the process is known as **artificial selection**. Desired changes in the phenotypic characteristics of an organism are achieved by **selective breeding**, that is individuals showing one or more of the desired features to a larger degree than other individuals are chosen for breeding. Some of the alleles conferring these features are passed on to their offspring. Again, the 'best' individuals from this generation are chosen for breeding. Over many generations, alleles conferring the desired charac-

teristics increase in frequency, while those conferring characteristics not desired by the breeder will decrease in frequency, or be lost entirely.

Selective breeding is carried out with many aims, including:

■ increasing the yield and nutritive value of crop plants;
■ increasing the growth rate, meat production, milk yield and egg production of livestock;
■ changing from fat to lean varieties of pigs, and other livestock, in response to consumer demand;
■ improving the performance of various animals, such as racehorses and homing pigeons;
■ producing new combinations of colours and scents in garden flowers;
■ producing particular characteristics in breeds of, for example, dogs, cats and birds;
■ producing pest-resistant and disease-resistant varieties of plants and animals;
■ producing plants and animals that are tolerant of environmental change in, for example, temperature or water supply.

It is important to realise that selective breeders have to consider the whole genotype of an organism, not just the genes conferring the desired characteristic, such as increased yield. Within the genotype are all the alleles of genes that adapt the organism to its particular environment. These genes are called **background genes**.

Suppose that the chosen parents come from the same environment and are from varieties that have already undergone some artificial selection. It is likely that the parents share a large number of alleles of their background genes, so the offspring will be adapted for the same environment.

Suppose instead that one of the chosen parents is from a different part of the world. The hybrid will inherit appropriate alleles of background genes from only one parent. It may show the trait being selected for, but may not be very well adapted to its environment in other respects. The same problem emerges if a cross is made between different species, for instance between a cultivated plant and a wild relative. (Although most true species are reproductively isolated from other species, some can be interbred to give fertile offspring. Such species are often those that do not normally come into contact with one another because they grow in different areas or habitats.) In such a cross, it is likely that the wild relative will contain alleles that are not wanted, and which had been selected out of the cultivated plant. The number of undesirable alleles of background genes derived from one parent can be decreased by repeatedly backcrossing to the other parent.

For example, in producing a new variety of potato for the United Kingdom, the breeder looks for a large number of different characteristics, including the yield and growth of the plant, the size, shape and colour of the tubers and the resistance of both plants and harvested potatoes to various pests. The desired characteristics are often derived from wild, South American strains of species related to the cultivated potato. These characteristics are very slowly bred into cultivated varieties using complex sequences of backcrosses. Note that the potato breeder in the United Kingdom faces a challenge, since the source of useful characteristics is not only from a different part of the world (and therefore has inappropriate background genes) but is also a wild species (with many unwanted characteristics, since it has undergone no artificial selection).

SAQ 2.1 _____

Unlike other major crops, oilseed rape varieties do not form a single species. Varieties are derived from five different species of *Brassica*. Apart from any difficulties that might be encountered in successfully fertilising one species with another, explain the challenge that faces the plant breeder in developing a new variety of oilseed rape.

The process of artificial selection was well known to Charles Darwin. He used examples of artificial selection in his book *On the Origin of Species* as an analogy from which his readers might understand the process of natural selection.

Both evolution and selective breeding result from changes in allele frequencies with time. The selective pressure in evolution is **natural selection**, whilst the selective pressure in selective breeding is the artificial selection that results from the breeder's choice of parents.

Selective breeding of plants

Plants with male and female flowers on different plants must cross-pollinate. Most crop plants are bisexual, and have both male and female parts in the same flower or both male and female flowers on the same plant. Such plants may, or may not, be capable of self-pollination. Plants such as wheat, peas and tomatoes, that normally self-pollinate are called **natural inbreeders**. Plants that must cross-pollinate are **natural outbreeders**. Examples of natural outbreeders include maize, apple and sunflower. Different techniques are used by plant breeders for natural inbreeders and outbreeders.

Inbreeders such as wheat may be selectively bred in different ways. These are shown in *figure 2.1*.

Single plant selection

Individual plants showing the desired trait are chosen and self-pollinated (selfed). The progeny of each plant is kept separate as a breeding line (usually planted out in a line, hence the name). The offspring are examined and again the best are selected and selfed. This process is continued for several generations. Genetic variation is reduced very rapidly, since each line derives from a single plant from the original population. Each pure-breeding line is a new variety.

Mass selection

A number of similar plants with the desired trait are chosen. As before, they are selfed and the best offspring selected and selfed. After several generations the pure-breeding lines are bred together as the new variety. Each line is genetically different. Hence, mixing the lines increases the genetic variation in the new variety.

Hybridisation

Parent plants from two inbred lines are chosen and cross-pollinated by hand. Since the plants normally self-pollinate, they must be prevented from so doing by removing the stamens before they mature (emasculation) or by making one inbred line male-sterile. (This may be done by introducing male sterility genes, by breeding, or by genetic engineering. Male sterility can also be produced by spraying with appropriate chemicals.)

When the stigmas are mature, pollen is transferred by hand. The flowers are isolated in bags both before and after pollination. The first generation of offspring (offspring 1) are all genetically identical. These are then selfed to give a second generation of offspring (offspring 2). At this stage, one of two procedures is adopted.

■ **Pedigree selection:** The best plants of the offspring 2 generation are selected and selfed and the process continued for several generations to give a new variety with the desired trait. Careful records are kept of the performance of each line, as the final selection is not only on the basis of the phenotype, but also on the plant's ancestry or pedigree: hence the name.

■ **Single-seed descent:** Alternatively no selection is applied to the offspring 2 generation. Instead, one seed, or a few seeds from each plant are grown and the plants selfed for several generations. Plants are grown at high density and

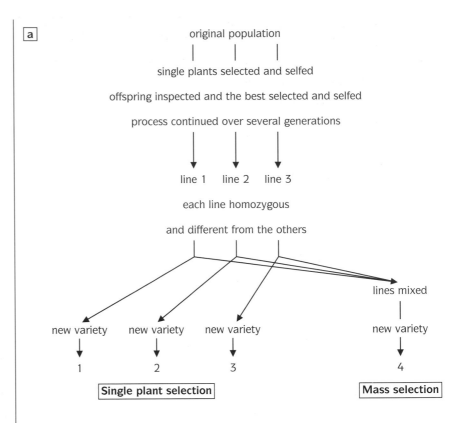

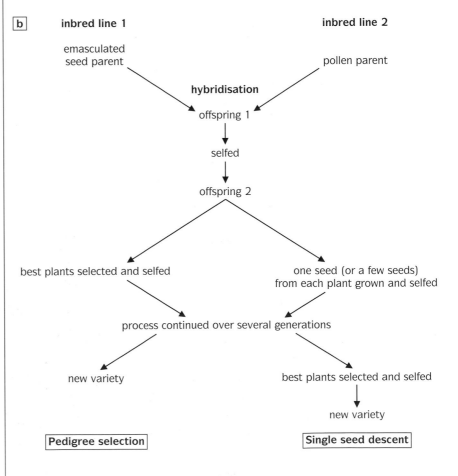

● *Figure 2.1* Different ways of selectively breeding wheat.

with low nutrient concentration in special rooms. This forces the plants to mature early, so that miniature plants of, for example, winter wheat, are produced in 18 weeks. Hence, three generations of winter wheat can be grown in a year. This cuts down the time needed to produce a new variety. Selection for the desired trait does not take place until about the sixth generation.

Each of these methods of selective breeding has advantages in particular circumstances, depending on species of inbreeder, time available and the characteristics undergoing selection.

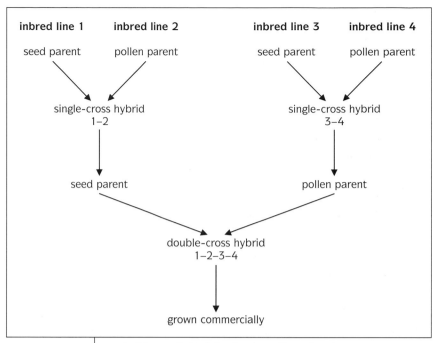

● *Figure 2.2* Selective breeding of maize.

SAQ 2.2

Examine *figure 2.1a* and suggest **one advantage** and **one disadvantage** to the farmer of growing 'new variety 4', resulting from mass selection, rather than 'new variety 1' which was produced by single plant selection.

A natural outbreeder is not tolerant of inbreeding. Inbreeding results in a reduction in size and yield, and a loss of vigour and fertility. This is called **inbreeding depression**. Crossbreeding two inbred lines commonly produces a hybrid that has a greater yield and is more vigorous than either of the parental lines. This is called **hybrid vigour**. You will meet both inbreeding depression and hybrid vigour again at the beginning of the next chapter. Selective breeding of natural outbreeders, such as maize, usually tries to make the most of hybrid vigour. A standard procedure is shown in *figure 2.2*.

Inbred lines are isolated to prevent cross pollination. Two inbred lines are then hybridised. Although a natural outbreeder, maize can self-pollinate and so must be prevented from doing so in order to produce a **single cross hybrid**. Until recently, the plants were emasculated by hand. In the United States alone, 40 000 people were employed in 1993, at a cost of millions of dollars, to go through plots of maize and remove the anthers. It is more usual now to make certain lines

male-sterile by means of male sterility genes.

Two more inbred lines are hybridised to give a second single-cross hybrid. Both single-cross hybrids have improved yields and vigour in comparison with their parental lines. However, yield can be increased still further by hybridising the two single-cross hybrids to give a double-cross hybrid.

Selective breeding of plants takes time and space (*figure 2.3*). A successful variety involves the screening of millions of potential varieties and may take up to 20 years to develop.

● *Figure 2.3* Trial plots of wheat at Plant Breeding International (Cambridge) Ltd, Cambridge, UK.

SAQ 2.3

Oilseed rape has no mechanisms to ensure, or to prevent, cross pollination. It is thought that between 30% and 50% of seeds are produced as a result of cross-pollination. Describe the precautions that must be taken, during a breeding programme, to prevent unknown pollinations.

Selective breeding of animals

In principle, plant and animal selective breeding is the same. In practice, however, animal selective breeders face several problems, particularly when dealing with mammals. Many of the mammals involved are large. They take time to reach maturity, gestation periods are long, and the number of offspring produced is small.

Some of the techniques of animal breeding which you will read about later, such as artificial insemination, embryo cloning and embryo transplantation, help to overcome these problems. However, in some breeding programmes, such techniques are never used. In the blood-stock industry, for example, a race horse stallion at stud (*figure 2.4*) covers 40 mares in a season lasting about five months of the year. Mares travel to the stud. If pregnant, they give birth there to the foals they are already carrying, and come into oestrus shortly after giving birth. The gestation period is eleven months. A stallion may go through four or five breeding seasons before anyone can tell if he is capable of siring winning progeny. A large number of mares, in comparison with stallions, is needed to produce a reasonable number of horses

to race in each successive season. This introduces a diluting effect on the selective breeding and the apparently intensive interbreeding of thoroughbreds has not, in fact, produced problems that suggest excessive inbreeding.

Progeny testing

The selective breeder has to choose appropriate parents for a cross. One criterion for that choice is the performance of an individual's progeny. Testing the value of an individual's genotype, in a particular breeding programme, by looking at the progeny produced by different matings is called **progeny testing**.

It is used in both plant and animal breeding, but is most important in animal breeding because of the number of commercially important characters, like milk production and egg laying, that appear in one sex only (sex-limited characters). For example, a bull cannot be assessed for milk production, nor a cock bird for egg laying. However, the performance of the animal's female offspring can be looked at to decide whether or not to use the animal for future crosses.

To perform a progeny test the male is crossed with a number of females with a proven performance. The average performance of the offspring is found, giving a measure of the male's value to the selective breeder.

Artificial insemination (AI)

Selective breeding of birds and mammals, including progeny testing, makes considerable use of artificial insemination. In artificial insemination, semen is placed into the female's vagina, or directly into the uterus in larger animals, using a catheter. Although not successful in some species of mammals, AI is extremely important in the selective breeding of cattle. The semen is commonly stored at $-196\,^{\circ}$C in liquid nitrogen. (You will find more information about sperm banks on page 28.)

● *Figure 2.4* Stallion and mare in breeding hall.

There are numerous advantages in the use of AI.

AI allows semen from one male to be used to fertilise a number of different females. This speeds up both progeny testing and selective breeding.

The farmer saves the cost of keeping a male animal, and the problems of running a male with a herd.

The costs and dangers of transporting animals for mating, and the stresses of mating, are all avoided.

AI is quickly available when needed.

Sperm can be sexed, and checked for certain genetic defects.

Sperm from different males can be used for different females, to avoid future inbreeding.

There are also disadvantages.

AI mostly uses frozen sperm, and low-temperature storage may damage sperm.

Should sperm from a particular male be used for a large number of inseminations, there is potential danger of future inbreeding, with its resulting problems (see page 24). Also, if it turns out that a male used to inseminate a large number of females has a genetic defect, the cost can be huge.

Also, since AI is an unnatural process, some people think that using it shows a lack of respect for animals.

AI in humans

Artificial insemination is also carried out in humans, to make it possible for some couples who are having difficulties in conceiving a child to have a baby. Artificial insemination of a woman with her husband's sperm (AIH) overcomes chronic impotence in men and fear of sexual intercourse in either sex. It may allow an otherwise infertile couple to have a child and introduces no third party into the relationship. This is seen as a problem only by those who disapprove of any intervention in the natural process of conceiving a child.

In some cases, the reason for the infertility is because the man cannot produce sperm or produces them in only very small numbers. Some of these couples will consider artificial insemination of the woman with sperm from a donor (AID). This will allow an otherwise infertile couple to have a child that is genetically the mother's, but not her partner's. The couple may see this as preferable to adoption of a child that is unrelated to either of them. Also, the woman carries the developing fetus and gives birth to her child.

However, AID introduces a third party into the couple's relationship and raises a number of social and ethical issues.

- A donor must not be used too often, in case of an unknown genetic defect, and in case half-siblings intermarry.
- There is a conflict between the need for anonymity of donors and the child's right to information about his or her genetic parent.
- AID allows women without a male partner to have a child. Many people regard it as undesirable for a child to be born to a lesbian couple or to a single woman who chooses to be so (rather than a woman who has lost her partner).
- A sperm donor should be free from known defects and from infections such as HIV. As more genetic tests become available (chapter 5), a potential donor might be under unreasonable pressure to undergo one or a number of these.
- Donor and recipient couple should 'match' in race, some physical characteristics, and, if necessary, religion. However, a choice of donor characteristics may be seen as a step towards unacceptable eugenics (that is selection for preferred human traits).

In vitro fertilisation (IVF)

Another technique that may be used in breeding mammals is that of in vitro fertilisation.

In vitro means *in glass*, because in vitro fertilisation takes place in a glass dish on a laboratory bench *(figure 2.5)*. IVF is used as a research tool in animal breeding and embryology, but is most commonly used in humans to treat women whose ovaries are functioning, but whose oviducts are blocked, preventing egg and sperm meeting in a

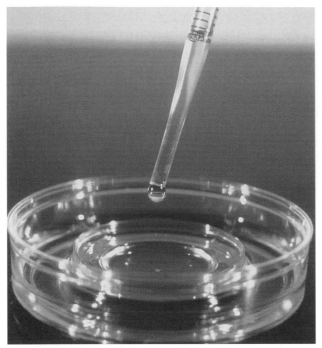

● *Figure 2.5* In vitro fertilisation: droplets of sperm are being added to a petri dish containing ripe oocytes.

normal fertilisation. It is also used where male infertility is due to low sperm motility. As you will see in chapter 5, IVF is also used in genetic screening.

In the IVF process, first a female mammal is treated hormonally so that several oocytes mature in each ovary at the same time. This is called **superovulation**. The female is artifically inseminated and the fertilised eggs are flushed out of the

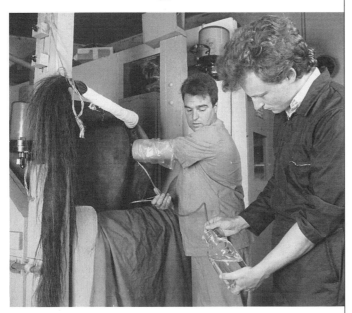

● *Figure 2.6* Flushing fertilised eggs out of a donor mare after artificial insemination.

uterus (*figure 2.6*). In humans, the ovaries are inspected by means of a fibre-optic light guide and the oocytes collected from their ripe follicles via a catheter. Eggs and sperm are then placed in a sterile nutrient solution and mixed for fertilisation to occur. If the activity of the sperm is poor, the outer 'wrapper' of the oocyte, the zona pellucida, is deliberately damaged to make it easier for sperm to penetrate. In other cases, sperm are placed inside the zona pellucida by microinjection, in a process called sub-zonal insemination (SUZI), or are put directly into the oocyte cytoplasm.

After fertilisation, the egg divides until it is a ball of 8–16 cells. At this stage the embryo is transferred to the uterus. Surplus embryos can be frozen and stored for implantation later, or donated to an infertile couple.

The success of IVF in humans is not high, but is rising. Currently, about 15–20% of the women treated at the larger centres in the United Kingdom become pregnant. A successful pregnancy is more likely if several embryos are implanted. In the United Kingdom this is limited to three by the Human Fertilisation and Embryology Authority's Code of Practice which regulates the conduct of infertility treatment and embryo research.

In IVF the oocytes, sperm, or the embryo itself can all be donated. **Gamete donation** involves ethical and social issues like those in AID. Oocytes are in very short supply, mostly coming from women themselves undergoing IVF. Donors undergo the hormone treatment necessary for superovulation. They should be under 35 years old to minimise the risk of genetic defects in the oocyte.

It is also possible to use eggs from ovarian tissue from aborted fetuses and from cadavers. However, after considerable public consultation, in 1994 the Medical Ethics Committee of the British Medical Association decided that fetal ovarian tissue should not be used to provide oocytes for infertile women, but that it can be used for research into infertility. Oocytes can be donated after death, if the donor has given specific permission, having understood what this would mean.

Embryo donation is essentially an early adoption by the recipient couple. The recipient mother carries and gives birth to the child, making it hers in everything except genetic origin.

What are the risks of IVF? The first baby born after IVF was Louise Brown, in the United Kingdom in 1978. In 1990, the *British Medical Bulletin* analysed nearly 1600 IVF births. This study showed that babies born after IVF were more likely to be premature, and were significantly lighter than babies conceived conventionally. Both of these effects are likely to be due to the increased number of multiple births resulting from IVF. No evidence of abnormality in development has been found.

Other concerns about IVF relate to the fate and ownership of 'spare' embryos. In the United Kingdom, embryos may be used up to 14 days after fertilisation for scientifically sound research. However, legislation on IVF and embryo research varies considerably across Europe.

Cloning and embryo transplantation

The ability to produce mammalian embryos in vitro, and to handle early embryos without damaging them, opens the way for cloning embryos and for transplanting embryos into surrogate mothers.

Cells of a mammalian early embryo are undifferentiated and the tissues they will eventually form is not yet determined. They are said to be **totipotent**, since each cell has the ability to produce a complete individual. Separating the two cells of a 2-cell stage embryo can result in identical twins. Carefully dividing a 16-cell or 32-cell stage into two clusters of cells also results in twins. The process can be repeated, giving a number of genetically identical individuals: a **clone**.

Experimental cloning of a human embryo was reported from the USA in 1993, but is banned in the UK by the Human Fertilisation and Embryology Authority.

Cloning livestock embryos is an important technique in animal breeding. Agriculturally important mammals, such as cattle, sheep and goats, are large. They have long gestation periods and small numbers of offspring. This restricts the rate of selective breeding. Cloning embryos and transferring them to surrogate mothers can overcome some of these problems.

A possible sequence of events in cattle breeding is shown in *figure 2.7*. A cow showing the characteristic(s) being selected for is chosen. She is treated with hormones, so that she superovulates. A suitable male is chosen. The female may be mated normally, or artificially inseminated. The resulting embryos are then washed from her uterus.

The embryos are transferred to the uteruses of recipient cows. These cows will have been treated hormonally so that their oestrus is synchronised with that of the fertilised cow and the uterus will be ready to receive an embryo. Two embryos are transferred to each surrogate mother. 'Spare' embryos may be frozen for later use.

The number of embryos can be increased by dividing them, growing them briefly in tissue culture, and then transferring them to surrogates. There are a number of advantages of this procedure in animal breeding:

- the reproductive rate of the genetically superior female is considerably increased;
- the genetically superior female is never put at risk by becoming pregnant;
- the transplanted embryos can be sexed and tested for certain genetic diseases before implantation;
- the embryos can be transferred to a small mammal, such as a rabbit, for transport around the world – the embryos are recovered and reimplanted into hormonally prepared surrogates;
- the surrogate may be from a different species: a horse may carry a zebra embryo, or a goat a guanaco embryo. This is particularly important when breeding rare animals.

Ethical objections can be raised against some or all of these procedures, in that the animals concerned are not only denied their natural instincts and behaviour, but are being used by the animal breeder as a means to an end.

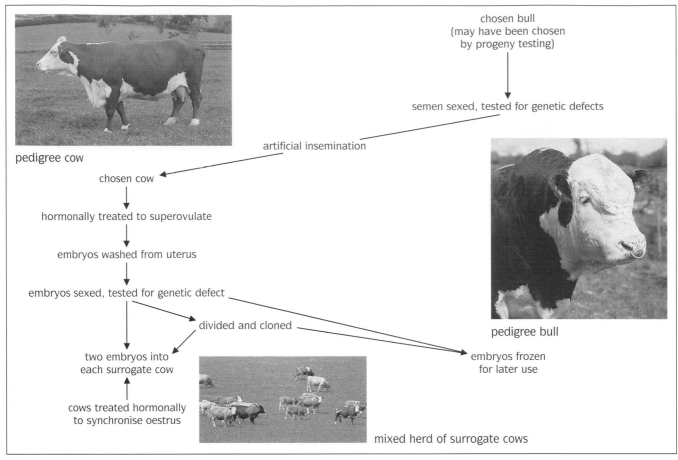

chosen bull
(may have been chosen
by progeny testing)

semen sexed, tested for genetic defects

pedigree cow

artificial insemination

chosen cow

hormonally treated to superovulate

embryos washed from uterus

embryos sexed, tested for genetic defect

divided and cloned

pedigree bull

two embryos into
each surrogate cow

embryos frozen
for later use

cows treated hormonally
to synchronise oestrus

mixed herd of surrogate cows

● *Figure 2.7* The use of embryo transplantation in cattle breeding.

SUMMARY

■ Selective breeding produces desired changes in the phenotype of an organism. Individuals showing the desired traits to a larger degree than other individuals are chosen for breeding. Selection over many generations increases the frequency of the alleles conferring the trait.

■ Both evolution and selective breeding result from changes in allele frequencies over time. The selective pressure in evolution is natural selection and in selective breeding is artificial selection.

■ Plants that normally self-pollinate are called natural inbreeders. Such plants can be selectively inbred to give pure-breeding varieties.

■ Plants that normally cross pollinate are called natural outbreeders and show inbreeding depression if inbred. Selective breeding of outbreeders commonly makes use of hybrid vigour.

■ Progeny testing looks at the performance of an organism's offspring and decides from that whether or not to select the organism for breeding. It is most often used in animals, particularly when selecting for traits that are sex-limited.

■ Artificial insemination involves placing semen into a female bird or mammal's reproductive tract by means of a catheter. It is important in cattle breeding, but not successful in all species of mammal. Artificial insemination in humans may be with sperm from the husband (AIH) or with sperm from a donor (AID).

■ In vitro fertilisation is fertilisation that takes place in a dish on the laboratory bench. Oocytes are collected from the female and mixed with a sample of semen. The fertilised egg undergoes mitosis and the resulting early embryo is transferred to the uterus of the genetic mother, or of a surrogate mother.

■ Early embryos can be subdivided to produce genetically identical clones.

Questions

1 Outline the principle of selective breeding and explain how this is carried out, with reference to named examples.

2 a Describe *two* examples of changes in organisms produced by selective breeding.
  b Discuss the similarity of selective breeding to the evolutionary process.

3 a Explain what is meant by *progeny testing*.
  b Describe, with examples, the way in which progeny testing is used in the selective breeding of animals.

4 a Explain the advantages and disadvantages of the use of artificial insemination (AI) in animals other than humans.
  b Discuss the social and ethical implications of the use of AI in humans.

5 a Describe the techniques used in embryo transplantation.
  b Discuss the social and ethical implications of the use of such techniques in humans.

Chapter three

Genetic diversity

By the end of this chapter you should be able to:

1 describe the harmful effects of inbreeding;

2 describe the maintenance and use of seed banks and sperm banks;

3 describe the process of cloning plants from tissue culture;

4 describe the genetic basis of resistance;

5 explain how selective breeding is used to produce disease-resistant varieties in plants and animals;

6 describe the development of antibiotic resistance in bacteria and pesticide resistance in insects and discuss the implications of the development of such resistance.

The sum total of all alleles of all genes in an inter-breeding population at a given time is referred to as that population's **gene pool**. Mutations add new alleles to the gene pool and increase genetic diversity, whilst natural selection and selective breeding tend to remove unwanted alleles from the gene pool and reduce genetic diversity. In this chapter you will meet examples of such changes.

The problems of inbreeding

Inbreeding results from the mating of closely related organisms. This may be a consequence of a small population or the result of selective breeding of either plants or animals. In plants described as 'natural inbreeders' (page 15), self-fertilisation is the usual method of sexual reproduction. Such plants can survive as very small, isolated populations. Inbreeding is also found in plant species which rapidly colonise new ground. These plants have the advantage that if only one or a few

individuals succeed in a new habitat, they can reproduce rapidly to give a large population, all of whose members will also succeed in that habitat. Inbreeding rapidly produces 'pure-breeding' lines that are homozygous at almost all loci so that the individuals of one line are phenotypically very similar. This may be exactly what the selective breeder wants. A natural inbreeder, such as wheat, is tolerant of this.

Outbreeding results from the mating of unrelated organisms. In nature, outbreeding is the norm in most animal species and many plant species. It ensures large genetic diversity in populations, allowing the population to respond to environmental changes. Species described as 'natural outbreeders', such as maize, are not tolerant of inbreeding *(figure 3.1)*, which causes a gradual decline in vigour, size and fertility. This is called **inbreeding depression**; the inbred line may die out.

Inbreeding depression is the result of an accumulation of deleterious recessive alleles. When the organism becomes homozygous for these recessive alleles because of inbreeding, the organism's **fitness** is reduced. (An organism's fitness is its ability to survive and reproduce in a particular habitat.) Such

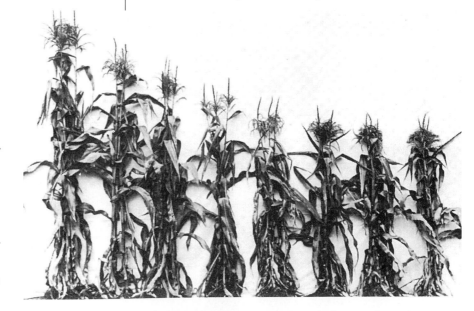

● *Figure 3.1* The effects of inbreeding depression in maize over 8 generations.

● **Figure 3.2** Hybrid vigour in maize. The hybrid in the middle was produced by crossing the two inbred varieties on each side. Compare the size of the hybrid with the parental varieties.

deleterious recessive alleles can reach quite high frequencies in a population of a natural outbreeder. This is because the organisms tend to be heterozygous at many loci through outbreeding, so the recessive alleles do not affect the phenotype and are not selected against. If these individuals inbreed, the offspring are more likely to be homozygous for one or more of these alleles and so less likely to survive and reproduce.

If inbreeding of a natural outbreeder is continued for many generations, fitness starts to increase again as the deleterious recessive alleles are gradually eliminated from the population. It can be assumed that natural selection has removed such deleterious alleles from the population of a natural inbreeder, and this is why it is tolerant of inbreeding.

In contrast, crossing two different highly inbred lines usually produces hybrids with more vigorous growth than either of the two parental lines. This phenomenon is called **hybrid vigour** or **heterosis**, and results from the large number of heterozygous loci that have been produced. The sequence of events is shown in *figure 3.2*. The answer to the

problem of inbreeding is outbreeding with an unrelated, genetically different organism. To find such an organism, the breeder may need the resources of a gene bank.

The need to maintain a gene bank

Genetic diversity in our crop plants and animals has made it possible to respond to changes in pests, diseases and climate, so that we continue to have food. Any future changes in such factors will place further demands on genetic diversity. Unfortunately, a number of factors (including selective breeding, modern agriculture, the growth of industry and of towns, and human population growth) have contributed to the extinction of many varieties and species of organisms. This is known as **genetic erosion** because it reduces genetic diversity.

It is important, therefore, to maintain as much genetic diversity as possible, so that if there is a climatic change, or if a new strain of a disease organism emerges, the breeder can find a suitable parent organism with the appropriate trait for breeding.

For example, the gene that increases the yield of about 80% of the wheat grown in the United Kingdom is a 'dwarfing' gene, derived from a Japanese variety of wheat, Norin 10. Because the stems are shorter, the wheat can be given large doses of nitrogen fertiliser without growing so tall that it falls over (or 'lodges'). The plant uses the extra nutrients to produce more grain. The gene also reduces the size of the grain, but increases the number of grains per ear. Provided the plant is well fed, overall yield is increased. When such plants are exposed to temperatures above 30°C before midsummer, the effect of the gene is altered, and the yield is decreased. With the possibility that global warming might increase average atmospheric temperature, wheat breeders are now looking for different 'dwarfing' genes, which they may find in a **gene bank**.

Gene banks store genes as the **genomes** (total genetic material) of cells, tissues or whole organisms. Despite the name, they are not stores of individual lengths of DNA. Gene banks include:

- wild populations of organisms;
- rare breeds of animals;
- crops in cultivation;
- botanic gardens and zoological gardens;
- seed banks;
- sperm banks;
- cells in tissue culture;
- frozen embryos.

Wild populations and rare breeds

The starting point in the conservation of crop plant diversity is to identify the so-called 'centres of diversity' for particular crops. A **centre of diversity** harbours the greatest genetic variation for a crop plant and its wild relatives. It is often found where the crop plant originated, for example potatoes and tomatoes in western South America. It is important that the genetic diversity of such centres of diversity is conserved for possible use in future breeding programmes.

As the number of breeds of livestock in common use decreases, because of selective breeding for particular characteristics in fashion at the moment, so genetic diversity disappears. In developed countries, each food or animal product has its own specialised animal. Generalist breeds are no longer kept on a large scale, as they are less profitable. Half of all the breeds that existed in Europe at the turn of the century have vanished and a third of the remaining breeds (approximately 770) are in danger of disappearing. The American Livestock Breeds Conservancy has listed 29 breeds that are threatened with extinction, of which 12 are unique to North America. Animals are 'listed' when there are fewer than 200 in North America and fewer than 2000 worldwide.

Competitive pressure from imported livestock is also threatening the genetic diversity of farm animals in developing countries. Aid programmes often aim to boost food production by crossing native breeds with imported animals, or by inseminating them with imported sperm. The United Nations Food and Agriculture Organisation (FAO) sends about 100 000 'doses' of cattle semen to developing countries each year. The FAO has now drawn up a conservation programme to encourage the breeding of endangered breeds in their homelands.

The requirements of breeders change, for instance in recent years lean meat has become preferable to fat meat, and it is not possible to predict what future requirements will be. Keeping rare breeds in existence conserves genes that may be needed in the future. Since different breeds derive from different parts of the world, they include an enormous variety of genetic material for adaptations to a wide variety of climates and diseases. It makes sense for us to conserve this variation in case of need.

Seed banks

The conservation, or 'banking', of most of the world's plant genetic resources depends on the state of 'suspended animation' shown by seeds. Most seeds remain viable for at least 15 years if they are carefully dehydrated until they contain only about 5% water and then stored at −20°C. With this small water content, there is little risk that ice crystals will form during freezing and so damage cells. Seeds that can withstand such dehydration and cooling are called **orthodox seeds**. It is estimated that 80% of plant species have orthodox seeds.

In general the storage life of a seed is doubled with every 5°C reduction in temperature, or by a reduction of 2% in the relative humidity. However, there are considerable differences in the storage life of different species. Cereal grains survive for very long periods: wheat taken from Ancient Egyptian tombs has been germinated successfully. Some other species also have seeds which are long-lived: in 1982, a magnolia seed excavated from an ancient Japanese settlement, and estimated to be 2000 years old, was germinated successfully.

About 20% of all plant species, and 70% of tropical plant species, have seeds that cannot be dried slowly and frozen. These are referred to as **recalcitrant seeds**. The seeds of many economically important tropical species, including rubber, coconut palm, cocoa and coffee, are recalcitrant. Oak and chestnut are examples of temperate species with recalcitrant seeds. The only way to preserve the genetic diversity of these species is to collect seed and grow each successive generation, or to keep them as tissue culture. However, work on the recalcitrant seeds of jackfruit has shown that if the embryo is dissected out of the seed and frozen slowly to −40°C, it remains viable. If this procedure can be applied to other recalcitrant seeds, a much greater proportion of the genetic diversity of these species will be kept more easily.

Seed storage is a very cost-effective method of banking genes *(figure 3.3)*. Seeds are mostly small and a large number can be kept in a small space. When collecting seeds to put into storage the aim is to include as great a range of genetic diversity as possible. The problem is to identify that diversity whilst collecting. Collectors sample a field crop more or less randomly, but are also asked to look out for phenotypic differences and to add seed from such plants to their random sample. They are also asked to take samples from land with different topography and from different climates and soils. Of course, some genetic diversity cannot be recognised from the phenotype, but DNA analysis can be used to identify this diversity. Collections are also made from areas of the world where vegetation is under threat.

The only way of finding out whether seeds in storage are still viable is to try to germinate them. It is recommended that seed banks carry out

● *Figure 3.3* Seed storage.

germination tests every five years. When the percentage of seeds that successfully germinate falls below 85%, the plants should be grown so that fresh seed can be collected and stored. It is necessary to know the particular conditions needed for germination of each species, and to be able to provide the correct conditions for the plants' growth if they are to produce seed for collection.

Whenever plants are grown from seed, there is the possibility of natural selection altering the particular mix of genes that was originally stored. Small samples of seeds from rare plants present a particular problem. Although a small sample may contain as much genetic diversity as a large one, it is more subject to random changes in gene frequencies as even smaller samples of the original are taken to test the seeds for viability, or to grow some plants in order to increase the number of seeds in store. Such samples are most unlikely to contain all the genetic diversity of the original sample. There is no simple answer to this problem, other than to put as large and diverse a sample as possible into store in the first place.

Different gene banks have worldwide responsibilities for different plant groups. The Genetic Resources Unit in Warwickshire has the responsibility of conserving the *Brassica* species (cabbage, cauliflower, etc.) and *Allium* species (onions, leeks, etc.). The International Rice Institute in the Philippines holds all rice varieties.

The genetic diversity of plant species whose seeds cannot be banked because they are recalcitrant, or which reproduce vegetatively, is stored in **field gene banks** (fields, orchards, plantations, botanic gardens) or in **tissue culture** (page 28). The major disadvantage of field gene banks is the space they occupy *(figure 3.4)*. The International Cocoa Genebank in Trinidad specialises in cocoa types from South America and grows 16 trees of each of the 2500 types of *Theobroma cacao* that it holds.

Coconut palms present a particular problem in banking. The seed is very large (the coconut); it is recalcitrant and the embryo is so large that it cannot be frozen satisfactorily. Collectors remove the embryos from the nuts and place them in sterile tubes. Later they are cultured and planted out.

● *Figure 3.4* A field gene bank of rice varieties at IRRI, Philippines.

Some tree species can be stored as frozen twigs, from which bud and root growth occurs after thawing.

Sperm banks and frozen embryos

There are a number of advantages of gene banks in the form of sperm banks or frozen embryos, rather than in the form of whole animals. Both occupy little space, and require little attention other than maintaining a low temperature. Both can be stored for long periods so that sperm from a particularly desirable animal and embryos from particular matings can be kept and used long after the death of the parent(s).

For a sperm bank, semen is collected (using an artificial vagina in some animals, such as cattle) and tested for motility. It is then diluted with an 'extender' medium which contains albumen and citrate buffer. The diluted semen is then put into small containers or 'straws', each containing enough semen for one insemination. These are stored at $-196\,°C$ in liquid nitrogen.

Frozen sperm has been successfully used in artificial insemination of cattle (page 18) for over a decade. But after years of research, farmers do not routinely use frozen ram or boar semen for breeding, because the success rate is too low.

Techniques to freeze eggs are not well advanced. Eggs are more difficult to freeze, because they:

■ are larger than sperm;

■ are spherical and hence have a small surface area/volume ratio and take longer than sperm to cool down;

■ do not have uniform cytoplasm and so freeze and thaw at different rates in different parts of the cell;

■ have chromosomes that are more vulnerable to damage than those of sperm because meiosis is not completed.

Embryos can be frozen successfully (page 21). The freezing of sperm and embryos is beginning to be used in contexts other than human reproduction and cattle breeding. For example, there are proposals to set up Europe's first 'frozen zoo'; a bank of frozen genetic material of endangered species.

Cloning plants from tissue culture

In the past, if a plant breeder wished to propagate a hybrid plant, a method of vegetative reproduction was used, such as taking stem, leaf or root cuttings. This is a relatively rapid way of reproducing a plant, but not all plants can be reproduced like this. Tissue culture is a method of vegetative reproduction on a massive scale. Within a few years several thousand plants, mostly identical to the original plant, can be produced. (Some mutation will occur, giving occasional variant plants.)

SAQ 3.1 _____

Explain why a plant breeder propagates a hybrid plant by vegetative reproduction, or by tissue culture, rather than allowing it to produce seed.

The process of tissue culture is now a routine procedure, and a number of commercial laboratories perform it as a service for plant breeders, for example in the propagation of hybrid *Dendrobium* orchids grown for the cut-flower market.

Young, developing orchid stems (called pseudo-bulbs) are removed from the parent orchid plant. The leaves are discarded from the pseudobulb and the stem surface-sterilised with a dilute solution of sodium chlorate (bleach). In sterile surroundings, small pieces of tissue (called **explants**) are placed in a sterile liquid medium containing mineral and organic nutrients, and plant growth regulators. (Solid media are used for many other species of plant at this stage.) The containers are sealed and placed on a shaking tray to keep the medium well-aerated. Undifferentiated cells in the explant, such as the meristematic cells of the cambium, divide by mitosis and produce a mass of undifferentiated tissue called a **callus** *(figure 3.5)*.

At this stage the callus can be subdivided to increase the number of plants eventually produced. Given appropriate plant growth regulators, the callus differentiates into tiny plantlets *(figure 3.6)*. These grow and when 5–10 cm long are transplanted into sterile soil. The transition from liquid medium to soil is the most difficult part of the process. The roots are very vulnerable to damage and infection and have to be treated carefully until they have had time to develop protection. The propagation of plants by tissue culture is also used after genetic engineering (chapter 4).

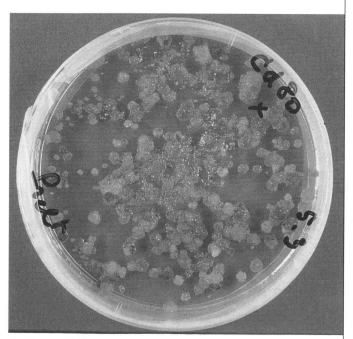

● *Figure 3.5* Petri dish containing plant tissue culture.

● *Figure 3.6* Plantlets growing in sterile culture.

The genetic basis of resistance

Cloning maintains a stable, genetically identical gene pool, except for the possibility of mutation. In the rest of this chapter you will find a series of examples involving the genetics of resistance: disease resistance in plants and animals, antibiotic resistance in bacteria and pesticide resistance in insects. These illustrate the effects of mutation and selection on the genetic diversity of a gene pool.

Disease resistance in plants and animals, and pesticide resistance in animals, may show discontinuous or continuous variation. It may be caused by single genes or by polygenes (page 2). Warfarin resistance in rats, which was described as an example of discontinuous variation in chapter 1, is controlled by a single gene. Crop plants with resistance to infection by fungi may have the resistance controlled by a single gene or by polygenes, as will be seen below. Some plants have resistance to one fungus controlled at a single locus, whilst showing polygenic control of resistance to another fungus, making their overall inheritance of resistance very complex.

Specific resistance

A crop plant which shows high resistance to one race of a species of pathogen, but low resistance to other races, is said to show specific (or vertical) resistance *(figure 3.7a)*. For example, flax may be attacked by different races of a fungus, *Melampsora lini*, causing flax rust. This was investigated by H. H. Flor in the USA in 1946 in a classic investigation into resistance. One variety of flax, Ottawa, is resistant to race 24 of *M. lini*, but susceptible to race 22. Another variety, Bombay, is susceptible to race 24 of *M. lini*, but resistant to race 22. When pure-breeding plants from each of the two varieties are interbred, the F_1 generation is resistant to both races of rust. Selfing the F_1 gives a 9:3:3:1 ratio of phenotypes, typical of a dihybrid cross.

One investigation into selfing the F_1 gave the following results:

Resistant to both races 22 and 24	Susceptible to both races 22 and 24	Resistant to race 22 but susceptible to race 24	Susceptible to race 22 but resistant to race 24
128 plants	14 plants	39 plants	44 plants

SAQ 3.2

Using appropriate symbols, state, with reasons, the genotypes of the parental varieties, Ottawa and Bombay.

The gene-for-gene concept

Flor's experiments led him to propose that the success or failure of infection is determined by single gene loci in both plant and fungus. In the fungus a gene codes for a protein involved in infection. The corresponding resistance gene in the plant codes for a specific receptor to the fungal protein. When a fungal protein interacts with its specific receptor, *no* infection occurs.

A mutation of the fungal gene, so that plant receptor and fungal protein no longer 'match', results in infection because the plant's resistance has been overcome.

General resistance

An organism showing general (or horizontal) resistance *(figure 3.7b)* has no specific resistance to a particular strain of pathogen, but has some resistance to a large number of different strains. This type of resistance is controlled by polygenes. Some varieties of wheat provide examples of specific resistance, whilst others show general resistance.

Selective breeding of disease-resistant varieties of plants: wheat

Until the 1960s plant breeders tried to produce resistant strains of wheat by introducing a succession of alleles of different genes, each of which gave resistance against a particular pathogen. However, each introduction of specific resistance was followed by chance mutations in the pathogen overcoming it. Breeders then recognised that selection for specific resistance was largely pointless. Fortunately, there were varieties of wheat (e.g. Maris Huntsman, first marketed in 1972) which, although attacked to some extent by most pathogens, showed general resistance.

Breeding programmes over the last 30 years have concentrated on breeding

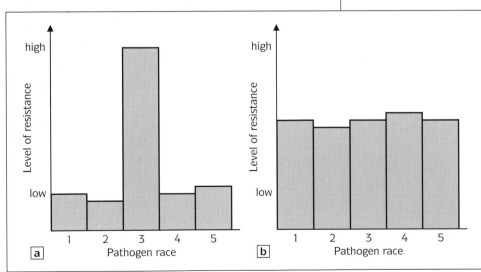

● *Figure 3.7*

a Specific or vertical resistance in plants. The plant has a gene locus giving resistance to pathogen race 3, but has only low resistance to the other races.

b General or horizontal resistance. The plant has no specific resistance but good general resistance.

for general resistance. For example Plant Breeding International (Cambridge) Ltd., Cambridge, UK, have produced a series of varieties of breadmaking wheats. The varieties Mercia, introduced in 1986, and Hereward, introduced in 1991, have high yields combined with general disease resistance. In the production of new lines, extensive tests are carried out. PBI Cambridge inoculates over 4000 wheat plots each year with *Fusarium* or *Septoria* to check for disease resistance or susceptibility.

Selective breeding of disease-resistant animals

Disease resistance in livestock is often not regarded as an important characteristic for selection in developed countries. The **heritability** (a measure of that part of the superiority of the parents which, on average, is passed to the offspring) of disease resistance is low. In developed countries, disease is controlled by vaccination, medication and by careful animal husbandry, rather than by selection. However, in developing nations, particularly in the tropics, disease control is more difficult and may be too expensive. In these circumstances, breeding disease-resistant animals is more important.

European breeds of cattle have undergone much more selection for traits such as high milk or meat yields than tropical breeds and, because of this, they have been introduced into tropical areas. However, a European breed of cattle introduced into the tropics is likely to be susceptible to local diseases and to be poorly adapted to the climate. The animals have the wrong background genes (page 14). Instead, tropical breeds of both dairy and beef cattle have been developed by making use of the appropriate background genes of *Bos indicus*, into which the desirable traits of European *B. taurus* have been introduced.

For example, the tropical milking breed of cattle, Siboney de Cuba, was produced by crossing Zebu (*B. indicus*) and Holstein (*B. taurus*) cattle. The Siboney de Cuba has approximately $\frac{3}{8}$ Zebu and

$\frac{5}{8}$ Holstein genes (*figure 3.8*), and is much more tolerant of various tropical diseases than is a European animal. Useful heterosis (page 25) occurs when the breeds of cattle being crossed differ markedly in their genotypes, as is the case here. The hybrid animals are likely to be heterozygous at a number of loci, giving some degree of hybrid vigour.

Another example of selection for disease resistance can be seen in sheep. Scrapie is a disease of sheep that has been endemic in the United Kingdom for more than 200 years. It is one of a group of transmissible diseases that affect the structure of the sufferer's brain, causing it to degenerate and acquire a characteristic spongy appearance. Some sheep are susceptible to scrapie; others are more resistant. In susceptible sheep, the incubation period for the disease is short and the animal succumbs to the disease, whereas in the more resistant sheep the incubation period is longer than the life span of the animal. The two types of sheep have different alleles of a gene called *Sip* (scrapie incubation period). The allele **pA** is associated with greater resistance and allele **sA** with susceptibility. Sheep with the genotype **sAsA** are more susceptible to scrapie than sheep with the genotype **pAsA**, which in turn are more susceptible than sheep with the genotype **pApA**. The different genotypes can be identified by analysing DNA (page 62) taken from blood samples. Once identified, resistant sheep can be interbred to produce a scrapie-resistant flock.

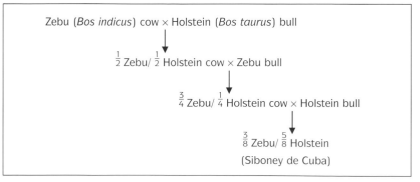

Zebu (*Bos indicus*) cow × Holstein (*Bos taurus*) bull

$\frac{1}{2}$ Zebu/ $\frac{1}{2}$ Holstein cow × Zebu bull

$\frac{3}{4}$ Zebu/ $\frac{1}{4}$ Holstein cow × Holstein bull

$\frac{3}{8}$ Zebu/ $\frac{5}{8}$ Holstein
(Siboney de Cuba)

● *Figure 3.8* The production of the tropical milking cattle, Siboney de Cuba, from Zebu and Holstein cattle.

SAQ 3.3

Explain why a flock of sheep bred in this way for resistance to scrapie may not be free from the agent that produces the disease.

Chickens differ in their resistance to different diseases and these differences are often the result of different alleles of a single gene locus. For example, inbred lines of chickens exist which differ in their susceptibility to infection by *Salmonella*. Research is in progress to develop DNA probes to identify different alleles of the *Sal* gene that give this resistance. Birds carrying the functional allele of the gene can than be selected for commercial breeding programmes. This would both improve the health and welfare of the birds and reduce the likelihood of *Salmonella* passing from infected chickens to humans who handle chicken meat or who eat inadequately cooked meat. In humans the bacteria cause the disease salmonellosis, which is a kind of food poisoning.

The development of antibiotic resistance in bacteria

The selective breeding of disease-resistant organisms shows the effects of artificial selection on genetic diversity, whilst the spread of antibiotic resistance in bacteria shows the effects of natural selection.

In addition to the circle of DNA that makes the bacterial chromosome (page 15, *Foundation Biology*), many bacteria contain small circles of double-stranded DNA called **plasmids** (*figure 3.9*). Plasmids carry genes which control their own replication,

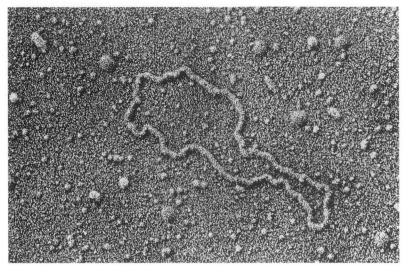

● *Figure 3.9* Electronmicrograph of a bacterial plasmid (× 125000).

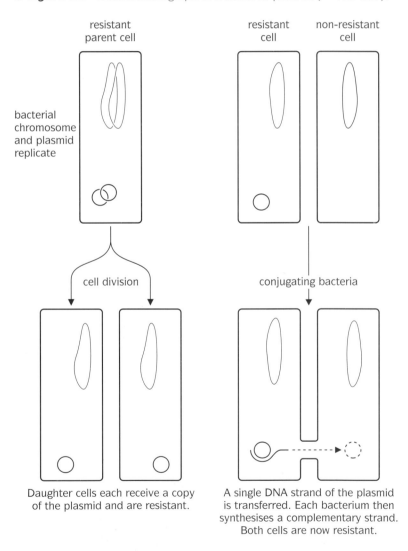

● *Figure 3.10* Vertical and horizontal transmission of resistance in bacteria.

so that they can replicate in the bacterial cell independently of the chromosome. Plasmids pass to new bacterial cells in two ways *(figure 3.10)*.

- When a bacterial cell divides, the two daughter cells each receive a copy of the bacterial chromosome and of a plasmid. This is **vertical transmission.**
- A bacterium may pass a copy of a plasmid to another cell in the process of **conjugation** *(figure 3.11)*. This is called **horizontal transmission.** The recipient bacterium may be of the same or of a different species.

In some circumstances plasmid DNA, and hence the genes carried by the plasmid, may be incorporated into the bacterial chromosome. DNA may also be transferred between bacteria by bacteriophage viruses (phages).

Plasmids may also carry genes that give the bacterium an advantage in particular circumstances, such as genes coding for enzymes that enable the bacterium to feed off unusual carbon sources, or for substances that improve the bacterium's ability to infect a host. Some genes can give resistance to an antibiotic, and these are carried on **resistance plasmids** or **R plasmids.**

An antibiotic is a substance produced by a living organism which either inhibits the growth of, or

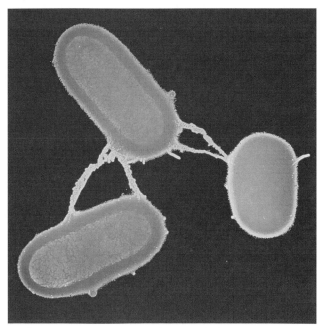

● *Figure 3.11* TEM of conjugation in *Escherichia coli* (× 17 500).

kills, bacteria. The antibiotic has its effect by blocking one or more enzyme reactions in the bacterial cell. Penicillin, for example, prevents the cross-linking of the molecules of bacterial cell walls. Other antibiotics work in other ways, by blocking either nucleic acid synthesis, or the transcription of DNA to RNA so that protein synthesis is stopped.

Resistance to an antibiotic arises in a bacterial population by chance mutation and is achieved in different ways. Resistance may be the result of:

- the presence of an enzyme that can break down the antibiotic;
- the presence of an enzyme that allows a different metabolic pathway to be used from that which is blocked by the antibiotic.

A bacterium with a gene giving resistance to an antibiotic has no advantage in the absence of the antibiotic. It is often at a disadvantage in comparison with a non-resistant bacterium, in that its different metabolism may be slower, resulting in a longer time between cell divisions and so a slower rate of increase in numbers. Also, the presence of the 'extra' genes, and the enzymes they code for, have a cost in the use of raw materials. In the presence of the antibiotic, however, resistant bacteria survive while non-resistant bacteria die. This is an example of natural selection, with the antibiotic acting as the selective agent.

Where there is widespread use of antibiotics, such as in hospitals and on farms, antibiotic resistance quickly spreads among different species of bacteria through conjugation (horizontal transmission). Resistance may first occur in a non-pathogenic bacterium but can then be passed to a pathogen.

R plasmids may carry resistance genes for several different antibiotics giving **multiple resistance.** R plasmids with up to 14 different resistance genes have been found.

Multiple resistance presents major problems

- A patient, suffering from an infection by a resistant strain of bacterium, and given the 'usual' antibiotic, may become seriously ill, or even die, before it is realised that the bacterium is resistant to that antibiotic. Another antibiotic, to which the bacterium is still susceptible, has then to be used.

■ A few antibiotics need to be kept as 'last resorts', to be given to patients suffering infection from multiple resistant strains of bacteria. When such antibiotics are used, however, there is the possibility of the bacterium developing resistance to it. Alternatively, a different bacterium may develop resistance, and this could spread to the multiple resistant variety by horizontal transmission. For example, multiple resistant *Staphylococcus aureus* (MRSA) shows resistance to four or more antibiotics. It can cause dangerous infection in hospital patients after surgery and is usually controlled by vancomycin. Now, strains of another bacterium, *Enterococcus*, have been found showing resistance to vancomycin. This raises the possibility that this resistance may be passed on to other bacteria, including MRSA.

It follows from this that there must be a constant search for new antibiotics. Possible new sources of antibiotics range from amphibian skin to shark tissues. However, there have been no important additions recently. Fortunately, a bacterium resistant to an antibiotic, for example penicillin, is often not resistant to that antibiotic with a slightly altered chemical structure. Chemists can make such **semisynthetic** antibiotics to extend the range available.

Reducing the problem of resistance

Obviously, we should try to reduce the occurrence of resistance. Ways of doing this include:

■ using antibiotics only when appropriate and necessary;

■ reducing the number of countries in which they can be sold 'over the counter' rather than prescribed, so that they are only used when needed;

■ avoiding the use of 'wide spectrum' antibiotics by using an antibiotic specific to the infection (provided that a correct diagnosis can be made);

■ ensuring that patients complete their course of medication;

■ taking antibiotics out of use to allow the incidence of resistant strains to decrease (this approach will not work if the resistance is carried by a multiple resistant strain which is still being selected for via one of the other antibiotics to which it shows resistance);

■ not adding antibiotics to animal feed to promote healthy growth of livestock.

An example of the danger of using antibiotics as growth promoters in livestock was shown in October 1994, when American microbiologists presented some evidence that genes for antibiotic resistance had moved from bacteria that live in the guts of livestock to related bacteria that live in human guts. The DNA sequences of 12 genes for tetracycline resistance (*tetQ*) from a bacterium, *Prevotella bacteroides*, which is found in farm animals, were compared with those from *P. intermedia*, found in the human mouth. All the *tetQ* genes had at least 94% of their DNA sequences in common in the two species of bacteria, and three genes shared 98% of their DNA coding. Most of the other genes of the two bacteria had only 10% of their DNA sequences in common. This is expected in species that diverged from a common ancestor a long time ago and whose DNA has since evolved along separate lines. The remarkable similarity of the *tetQ* genes suggests a very recent and frequent transfer from one species to another.

SAQ 3.4

Explain why the failure of patients to complete a course of antibiotics encourages the development of bacterial resistance to antibiotics.

The development of insecticide resistance in insects

Chemicals have also been used on a large scale to control insects. The insecticide DDT (dichloro-diphenyl-trichloro-ethane) was first used in Europe in the 1940s. By 1948, strains of flies that were resistant to several hundred times the normal dosage of DDT had been found in both Sweden and Italy. Within a few years resistant insects were reported in many countries. Farmers turned to other, related chemicals such as prolan and lindane, only to find that resistance to those soon built up as well (*figure 3.12*).

The pattern has been repeated for one insecticide after another and is an example of selection. The insecticide acts as the selective

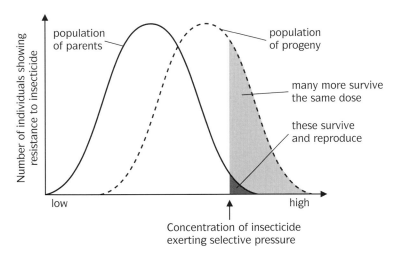

● *Figure 3.12* Graph of insecticide resistance in insects.

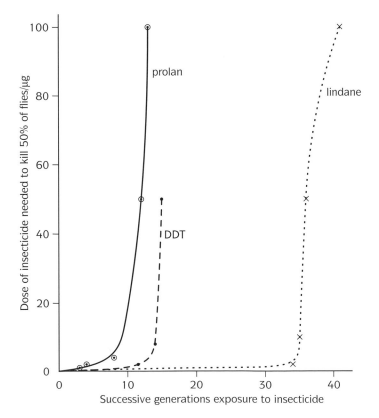

● *Figure 3.13* Graph showing the increasing concentration of insecticide needed to kill insects.

agent. The more an insecticide is used, the greater the chance of selecting for resistant insects. So if a new insecticide is introduced and farmers lavish it on their crops, among the very large number of insects treated a few will, by chance, be equipped genetically to survive the concentration of insecticide used. The resistant insects will survive and contribute more offspring than non-resistant insects to the next generation, and pass on the genes that give resistance. As each new generation is produced, the insect population will become more resistant to the insecticide so that it takes more insecticide to kill the insects (*figure 3.13*). This is expensive and may damage the crop, kill natural predators of the pest and harm other animals in the environment.

Now, more than 500 species of insect show resistance to at least one chemical. Increasing numbers of species are resistant to several insecticides. There is a real danger that the appearance of resistant strains will outstrip the production of effective insecticides.

No insect is totally resistant to an insecticide, even when it is resistant to the concentration that can safely be applied without affecting the plant. There is sometimes a relatively small margin between the concentration of insecticide that kills an insect and that which damages the crop plant. The genetics of resistance in insects is complex, and usually involves several loci, often with multiple alleles with additive effects (page 4).

SAQ 3.5

The Australian sheep blowfly *Lucilia cuprina* can develop resistance to the organophosphorus insecticide diazinon. There are four possible alleles at the Rop(resistance to organophosphorus)-1 locus, of which one results in susceptibility to diazinon, whilst the other three (Rop-1^A, 1^B and 1^C) give different, additive levels of resistance. The relative levels of resistance of the four possible homozygotes is shown in *table 3.1*.

Alleles for resistance	Relative level of resistance of fly
none (susceptible)	1.0
Rop-1^A Rop-1^A	9.0
Rop-1^B Rop-1^B	4.8
Rop-1^C Rop-1^C	7.7

● *Table 3.1*

a State the number of possible genotypes with respect to this locus and suggest whether the possible phenotypic variation in resistance level is likely to be discontinuous or continuous.

b Predict the level of resistance of flies heterozygous at the Rop-1 locus with the following genotypes:

Rop-1^A Rop-1^B
Rop-1^B Rop-1^C
Rop-1^A Rop-1^C.

There is a group of naturally occurring toxins which are formed in the spores of the soil bacterium *Bacillus thuringiensis*. When these are eaten by insects, such as leaf-eating caterpillars or fly larvae, those insects which have the correct enzymes digest the toxin to toxic proteins and are killed. Since each toxin is specific to one kind of insect, this means there is less chance of affecting non-target species. Also, because they are natural insecticides, it was thought that the target species would be less likely to develop resistance to them as they do to chemical insecticides.

More than 50 of the toxins have been identified so far, with specific targets including butterfly and moth caterpillars, mosquito larvae and beetle larvae. Insecticide sprays based on these toxins have been used for more than 20 years in a few countries and their use has increased considerably since the mid 1980s. Most commercial sprays contain a mixture of different *B. thuringiensis* toxins, because it has been assumed that the chance of an insect showing resistance to all the toxins at the same time would be negligible. However, isolated populations of insects showing such multiple resistance have been found. Indeed, laboratory experiments that involve breeding successive generations of insects exposed to the toxins have shown that a wide range of insects have the capacity to produce resistance. The danger of resistance developing has also been increased by the introduction of the genes for the toxins directly into plants through genetic engineering (page 47). (For more information on *B. thuringiensis*, see *Microbiology and Biotechnology* in this series.)

The main ways in which we can reduce the build-up of insecticide resistance in insect populations include:

■ using narrow-range (specific) insecticides rather than broad-range ones such as DDT, prolan and lindane;
■ spraying an insecticide only when necessary;
■ using high enough concentrations of insecticide to kill partially resistant insects;
■ varying the pesticide used so as to delay the evolution of resistance to a particular insecticide;
■ leaving unsprayed 'refuges' so that the effects of selection on the sprayed population is diluted by insects that have not been subjected to selection;
■ planting, close to a crop, a variety of plant which attracts the pest more, as a 'trap crop' which can be sprayed with insecticide killing a large percentage of the pest population;
■ using biological control, that is the artificial control of a pest species by means of another organism that is a predator or parasite of the pest (see *Ecology and Conservation* in this series).

Note that using high concentrations of insecticide may select for resistance very quickly, since any insect that survives will show a high level of resistance. Also many farmers will be reluctant to leave 'refuges', in which the pest is eating the crop and decreasing the yield, in the hope of some long-term gain.

SAQ 3.6

Figure 3.14 shows how the level of resistance to an insecticide of a malarial vector, *Anopheles albimanus*, in El Salvador varied between 1970 and 1972 in relation to the use of the insecticide in agriculture. During 6 months of each year the insecticide was sprayed onto cotton crops. No spray was used in the intervening periods.

Account for:

a the rise in the level of insecticide resistance of *A. albimanus* during the periods when spraying took place;

b the difference in level of insecticide resistance of the insect population at the ends of the two periods of spraying;

c the fall in level of insecticide resistance of the insect population when no spraying occurred.

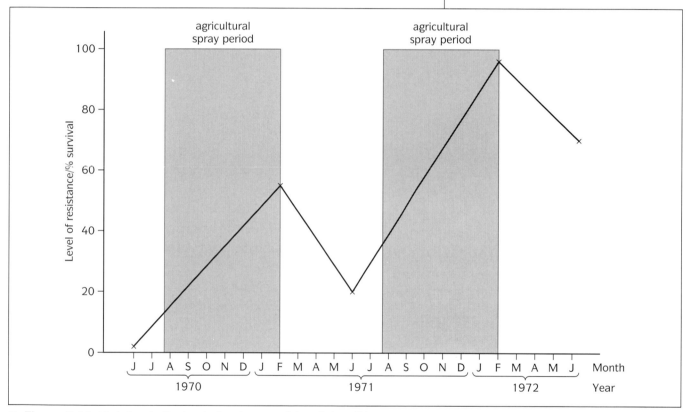

● **Figure 3.14** Variation in the level of resistance of *Anopheles albimanus* to an insecticide in relation to its use.

SUMMARY

- Inbreeding is the mating of closely related organisms; outbreeding is the mating of unrelated organisms. A natural inbreeder is tolerant of inbreeding, but a natural outbreeder shows a decline in vigour, size and fertility if inbred. This is called inbreeding depression. It is caused by an accumulation of deleterious recessive alleles.

- Hybrid vigour (heterosis) is the increased vigour achieved by crossing two inbred varieties.

- A gene bank is a store of genetic variation that may subsequently be called upon by plant or animal breeders to introduce a particular character into their breeding stock. Plant variation is banked as seeds, as growing plants and as tissue culture.

- Orthodox seeds can be dehydrated and then stored at low temperature. Recalcitrant seeds cannot be kept in this way.

- Undifferentiated plant tissue can be grown in sterile nutrient medium to form a mass of undifferentiated cells called a callus. This can be subdivided, and eventually differentiated to form large numbers of genetically identical plantlets.

- Animal variation is banked as living animals, as sperm banks and as frozen embryos. Sperm is stored in an extender medium in small 'straws' at $-196\,^{\circ}C$.

- Disease resistance in plants may be controlled by single gene loci or by polygenes. A plant which has high resistance to one race of a pathogen, but low resistance to others, is said to show specific (vertical) resistance which is controlled by a single gene locus. A plant which has some resistance to a large number of strains of pathogen is said to show general (horizontal) resistance. This type of resistance is controlled by polygenes.

- Selective breeding is used to produce disease-resistant varieties of plants and animals.

- Genes that give bacteria resistance to a number of antibiotics are carried on R plasmids. Plasmids may be passed 'vertically' to daughter cells, or 'horizontally' to other bacteria. Resistance arises randomly by mutation and spreads in a bacterial population by natural selection. The antibiotic acts as a selective agent.

- Pesticide resistance in insects also arises randomly by mutation and spreads in an insect population by natural selection. The pesticide acts as the selective agent.

Questions

1 a Describe, with examples, the problems which arise from inbreeding.
  b Explain how these problems may be overcome.

2 Outline the use in selective breeding of:
  a seed banks, b sperm banks, and
  c wild species.

3 a Describe how gene banks are established for plants and animals.
  b Discuss, with examples, the advantages of maintaining gene banks.

4 Describe the process of cloning plants from tissue culture.

5 a Explain the genetic basis of resistance.
  b Discuss, using specific examples, how selective breeding can produce disease-resistant varieties in plants and animals.

6 a Describe how antibiotic-resistant strains of bacteria arise.
  b Suggest how the spread of antibiotic resistance in bacteria can be controlled.

7 a Explain how pesticide resistance has arisen in insects.
  b Discuss the implications of the evolution of such resistance.

Genetic engineering

Organisms can be modified by genetic engineering

The aim of genetic engineering is to remove a gene from one organism and transfer it into another in such a way that the gene is expressed in its new host. The host is now described as **transgenic**. Genetic engineering provides a way of overcoming barriers to gene transfer between species. Indeed, the gene in question has often been taken from an organism in a different kingdom: such as a bacterial gene put into a plant, or a human gene into a bacterium. Unlike selective breeding, where whole sets of genes are transferred, genetic engineering results only in the transfer of single genes.

There are many different ways in which a transgenic organism may be produced, but certain steps are essential. The genetic engineer must:

■ obtain the wanted gene;
■ clone the gene to produce many copies;
■ insert a copy of the gene into the host DNA.

Obtaining the wanted gene

There are three different ways of obtaining a particular gene.

■ Firstly, provided that the amino acid sequence of the protein produced by the gene is known, the DNA code for the gene can be worked out and the DNA made in the laboratory. Many proteins are so large that even if their amino acid sequence is known, manufacture of the gene would be very tedious. However, automated machines are making this approach easier.

■ Another approach involves isolating the messenger RNA (mRNA) that has been transcribed from the wanted gene and making a DNA copy of the mRNA. One example of the use of this approach is the manufacture of insulin. Gland cells are specialised to produce one or more particular products, often in large quantities, for example some cells of the human pancreas produce insulin. These cells contain many copies of insulin mRNA which are translated into insulin by the ribosomes in the cell. The mRNA can be isolated and complementary single strands of DNA (cDNA) produced, by using the viral enzyme **reverse transcriptase**. The single-stranded cDNA is then made into double-stranded DNA by allowing the enzyme **DNA polymerase** to make a second strand of nucleotides with bases complementary to those of the cDNA. Each of the resulting DNA molecules is a copy of the insulin gene.

■ A third method involves isolating a gene from an entire genome. To do this, the total DNA of the genome is first cut into fragments, one of which must be identified as containing the wanted gene (page 41). The enzymes used to fragment DNA are called **restriction enzymes**.

Restriction enzymes

Restriction enzymes (restriction endonucleases) are a class of enzymes from bacteria which recognise and break down the DNA of invading bacteriophages (phages). These phages are viruses that parasitise bacteria. Bacteria with restriction enzymes can successfully 'restrict' infection by phages. Each restriction enzyme binds to, and cuts, foreign DNA at a specific target site. (The bacterium's own DNA is protected from such attack, either by chemical markers or by not having the target sites.)

Restriction enzymes are named by an abbreviation which indicates their origin. Roman numbers are added to distinguish different enzymes from the same source. For example, EcoRI comes from *Escherichia coli* (strain RY13) and is the first to have been identified from this source; HindIII is the third enzyme identified from *Haemophilus influenzae*.

The target site on the DNA is usually between four and six base pairs long. The target sites of some restriction enzymes are shown in *table 4.1*. Note the symmetry of the target sites: they are palindromic. Note also that both strands of the DNA may be cut in the same place (e.g. by HpaI) or in different places (e.g. by BamHI) leaving so-called **sticky ends**.

Figure 4.1 shows how sticky ends may be produced and used in genetic engineering. A circular strand of DNA, of a virus or of a bacterial plasmid, is cut using EcoRI. The DNA has only one target site for the enzyme, so the

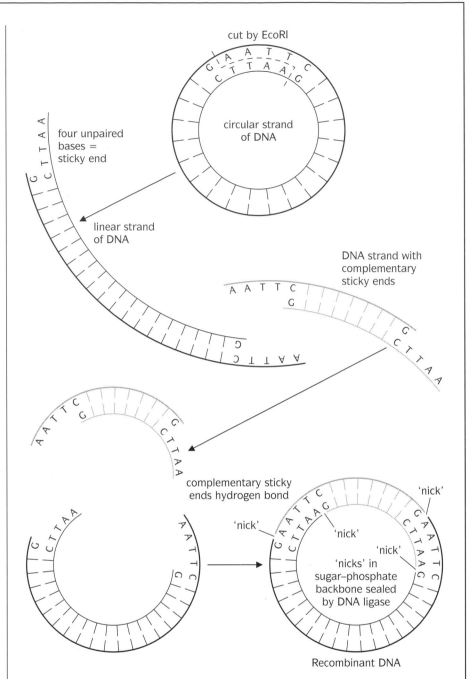

● *Figure 4.1* The production and use of sticky ends.

Enzyme	Target site
BamHI	G↑G A T C C C C T A G↑G
EcoRI	G↑A A T T C C T T A A↑G
HindIII	A↑A G C T T T T C G A↑A
HpaI	G T T↑A A C C A A↑T T G
HpaII	C C↑G G G G↑C C

● *Table 4.1* Target sites of various restriction enzymes

circular strand becomes a linear molecule with four unpaired bases at each end. These unpaired bases can bond with their complementary bases, either with the other end of the strand to make a circle again, or with another strand of DNA which has complementary sticky ends. Being able to join together different pieces of DNA is an important technique in genetic engineering. Such hybrid DNA, of different origins, is called **recombinant DNA**.

When two complementary sticky ends of DNA bond there are gaps, called **nicks**, left in the sugar–phosphate backbones of the DNA strands. Each gap is sealed by the addition of a phosphate group by the enzyme **DNA ligase**.

DNA strand with no sticky ends

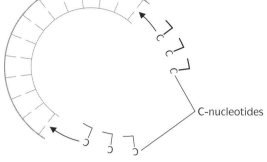

C-nucleotides

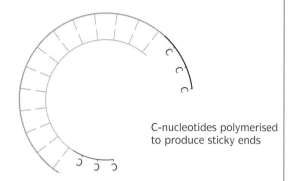

C-nucleotides polymerised
to produce sticky ends

● *Figure 4.2* Creating sticky ends.

If DNA does not have sticky ends, because it has been cut by HpaI or is a cDNA strand, these can be provided by adding single chains of nucleotides with, for example, cytosine (C) bases, to each end of the molecules *(figure 4.2)*. This is done by mixing the DNA with a supply of cytosine nucleotides and the enzyme **terminal transferase**.

SAQ 4.1

The restriction enzyme EcoRII cuts DNA at the target site G*C–C–T–G–G–C. The cut is made at the point marked *. Show the sticky ends that are produced by EcoRII when it cuts a DNA strand that contains the target sequence.

A restriction enzyme, such as BamHI, cuts DNA at every point at which its target site occurs, scissoring the genome into fragments of various lengths. Only one of these lengths will contain the wanted gene *(figure 4.3)*. In order to identify and clone the gene, the fragments are next inserted into **vectors**.

Vectors

A vector is a carrier DNA molecule into which a DNA fragment containing the wanted gene can be inserted. The result is a molecule of recombinant DNA. Different vectors are used in genetic engineering, depending on the size of the DNA fragment to be incorporated, and on the source and future fate of the DNA.

Viral DNA may be used as a vector for cloning small DNA fragments. The viral DNA may be circular or linear and is broken in a non-essential part of the genome so that the wanted DNA fragment can be inserted. The virus can then be replicated by its host cell, producing many copies of the recombinant DNA. Lambda (λ) phage, which is replicated by bacterial cells, is commonly used as a vector to insert genes into *E. coli*. However, the length of DNA that can be added to λ phage is limited, because of packing the DNA into the virus.

It is sometimes necessary to use a eukaryotic host cell to clone recombinant DNA, either because of the size of the DNA or in order to have the appropriate responses to the gene 'switches'. **Yeast artificial chromosomes (YACs)**, first constructed in 1987, are the largest size of vector. These are used for cloning mammalian or insect

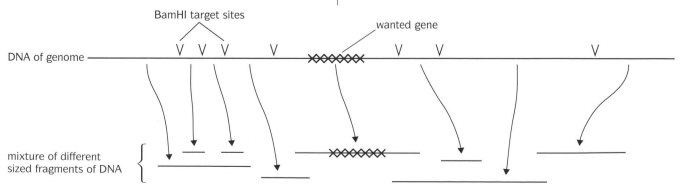

● *Figure 4.3* Fragmenting the genome with a restriction enzyme.

genes that are larger than 100 000 base pairs.

The most commonly used vector is a bacterial **plasmid**, which is a small circle of DNA. It is common to use a plasmid with genes coding for resistance to two antibiotics as these are useful in identifying recombinant DNA (page 00).

The plasmid pBR322 *(figure 4.4)* has been manufactured as a vector. It carries genes coding for resistance to ampicillin and tetra-cycline, and has single target sites for several restriction enzymes. Most of the target sites are within one of the resistance genes, so that cutting the DNA within one of the resistance genes, and inserting a DNA fragment, inactivates that resistance gene. This is important for identifying colonies, as you will see below.

The stages in extracting and cloning a particular gene are as follows.

Step 1: The genome is cut into fragments by BamHI and mixed with a sample of pBR322 which has also been cut with BamHI. This means that the sticky ends of the DNA frag-ments of the genome and of the plasmid are the same. The sticky ends of the mixture will join up in three different ways *(figure 4.5)* giving circular frag-ments of the genome, unaltered plasmids and recombinant plasmids. Some recombinant plasmids will contain the wanted gene.

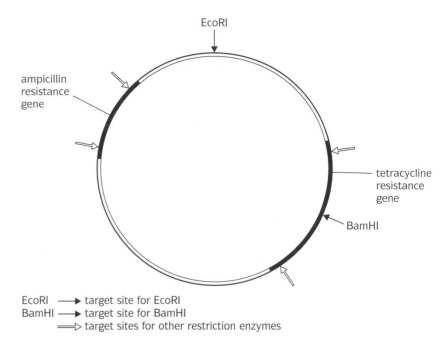

EcoRI ⟶ target site for EcoRI
BamHI ⟶ target site for BamHI
⟹ target sites for other restriction enzymes

● *Figure 4.4* The pBR322 plasmid.

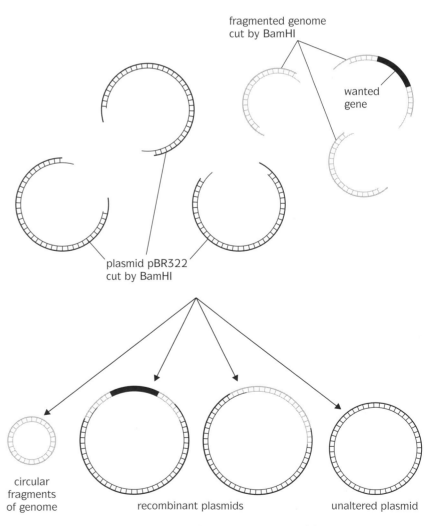

● *Figure 4.5* Mixture of genome fragments and pBR322 cut with BamHI.

Step 2: Bacteria, such as *E. coli*, can take up plasmids in the presence of calcium ions, so the mixture produced in Step 1 is added to a growing culture of bacteria, together with some calcium chloride solution. A small proportion of bacteria (about 1%) will take up DNA. The next problem is to identify which bacteria have taken up the wanted gene.

Step 3: The bacteria are transferred to culture plates containing ampicillin. Only those bacteria that have taken up a plasmid with the gene coding for ampicillin resistance will survive. These include bacteria that have taken up unaltered plasmids and recombinant plasmids, but not those that took up circular fragments of the genome.

Step 4: The bacterial colonies growing on plates containing ampicillin are now replica plated *(figure 4.6)* onto plates containing tetracycline. Bacteria that have taken up recombinant plasmids cannot grow in the presence of tetracycline since the gene conferring resistance has been inactivated.

By comparing the two plates, any colonies that are resistant to ampicillin, but killed by tetracycline, can be identified. Those bacteria contain a recombinant plasmid.

SAQ 4.2

Explain why, in the above procedure, bacteria which have taken up unmodified pBR322 are resistant to both ampicillin and tetracycline; those which have taken up recombinant plasmids are resistant only to ampicillin, and those that have not taken up a plasmid are resistant to neither antibiotic.

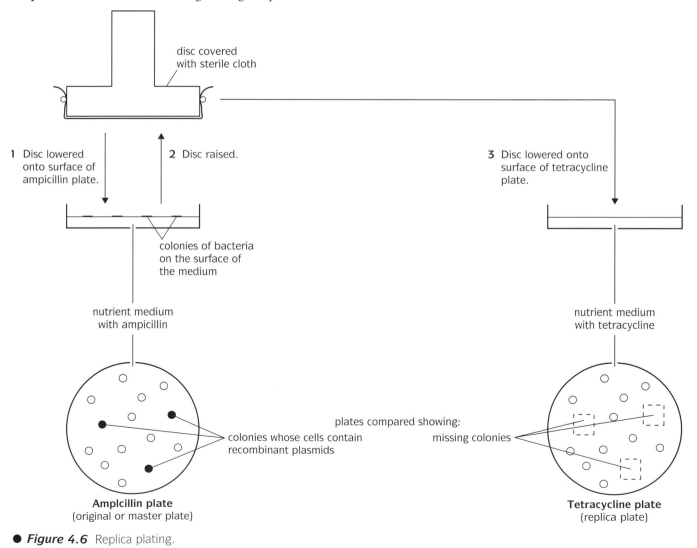

1 Disc lowered onto surface of ampicillin plate.

2 Disc raised.

3 Disc lowered onto surface of tetracycline plate.

disc covered with sterile cloth

colonies of bacteria on the surface of the medium

nutrient medium with ampicillin

nutrient medium with tetracycline

plates compared showing:

colonies whose cells contain recombinant plasmids

missing colonies

Amplcillin plate
(original or master plate)

Tetracycline plate
(replica plate)

● *Figure 4.6* Replica plating.

Provided that at least one copy of every DNA fragment that was originally produced by cutting the genome is present in one or more colonies, these make up a **gene library** of the genome.

One problem remains: that of sorting out which colony (or colonies) contain the DNA fragment containing the wanted gene. For this we need a **gene probe** (*box 4A*).

Step 5: The DNA of the gene that we are searching for has to be made single-stranded so that a gene probe can bind with it. A porous membrane or filter is placed on top of the plate of bacterial colonies. After 1–2 days, the filter, now carrying a sample of each colony, is removed. The filter is baked to kill the bacteria, and treated with alkali to denature the DNA into single strands.

Now the gene probe is added. Wherever the probe finds a complementary sequence of DNA, it binds. Excess probe is washed off and the binding sites detected by their radioactivity. The position of these sites on the filter corresponds to the positions on the culture plate of the bacterial colonies that contain the wanted gene. These colonies can be isolated and multiplied.

At last, there is a supply of many copies of the wanted gene.

Inserting a gene into a host

When the host cell that is to express a foreign gene is a bacterium, the gene is normally inserted into the cell by incorporating it into a plasmid, using the techniques described above. The genetically engineered bacteria are then cultured on a large scale in order to harvest the product of the gene. A good example of this is the production of human insulin by the bacterium *Escherichia coli*, which is described in *Central Concepts in Biology* and summarised in *figure 4.8*.

Another method of inserting foreign DNA into a cell is by **microinjection** (*figure 4.7*). This was the first technique to be used. Other 'direct' methods include:

- **electroporation**, in which rapid, brief electrical pulses produce temporary holes in the cell surface membrane of a cell through which DNA can be taken up;
- **microprojectiles** – tiny beads of tungsten or gold are coated with the required DNA and fired at cells by means of an explosive charge in a 'gun'.

Such direct methods of inserting DNA apply only to isolated cells or cells in tissue culture. Methods of introducing DNA into many cells in an animal include using viruses as vectors, or putting the DNA into liposomes. Liposomes are small spheres of phospholipid bilayers (chapter 5, *Foundation Biology*). These can fuse with the cell surface membrane of a cell and release the DNA into the cell. These will be looked at again in chapter 5.

These methods of inserting DNA merely introduce it into a cell. They do not insert the gene into the host genome. The all-important vector for

---

Box 4A Gene probes

Provided part of the base sequence of the gene is known, a short length of single-stranded DNA can be manufactured (about 20 nucleotides long) that is identical to part of the base sequence of one of the DNA strands of the gene and complementary to the other. The probe is radioactively labelled by using nucleotides that contain ^{32}P.

The probe will bind to single-stranded DNA with the complementary base sequence, and its presence detected by its radioactivity.

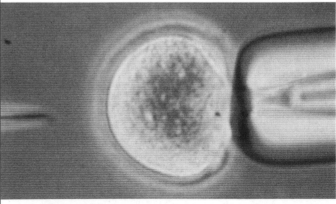

● *Figure 4.7* Photomicrograph of microinjection of DNA into a fertilised mammalian egg. The cell is held steady by the suction tube on the right, while the probe on the left introduces the DNA.

Isolation of human gene

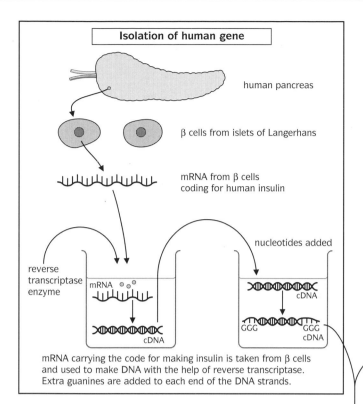

human pancreas

β cells from islets of Langerhans

mRNA from β cells coding for human insulin

reverse transcriptase enzyme

nucleotides added

mRNA carrying the code for making insulin is taken from β cells and used to make DNA with the help of reverse transcriptase. Extra guanines are added to each end of the DNA strands.

Preparation of vector

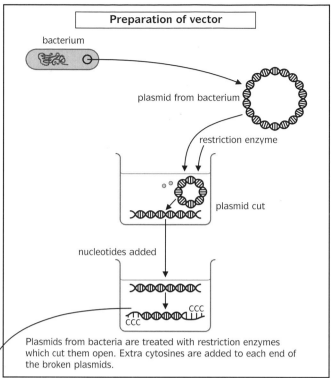

bacterium

plasmid from bacterium

restriction enzyme

plasmid cut

nucleotides added

Plasmids from bacteria are treated with restriction enzymes which cut them open. Extra cytosines are added to each end of the broken plasmids.

Formation of recombinant DNA

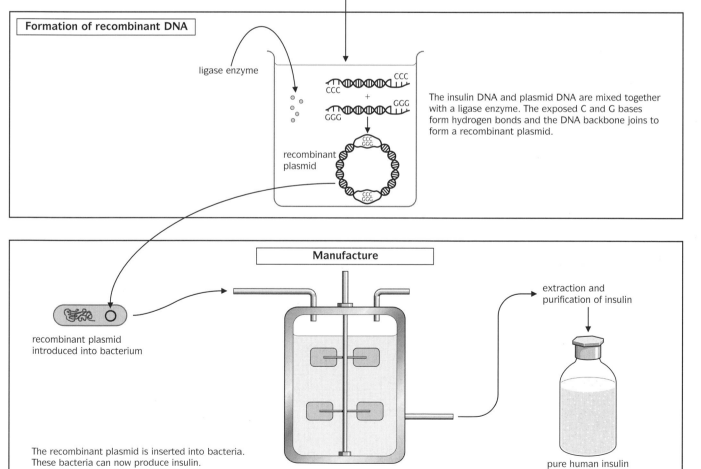

ligase enzyme

recombinant plasmid

The insulin DNA and plasmid DNA are mixed together with a ligase enzyme. The exposed C and G bases form hydrogen bonds and the DNA backbone joins to form a recombinant plasmid.

Manufacture

extraction and purification of insulin

recombinant plasmid introduced into bacterium

The recombinant plasmid is inserted into bacteria. These bacteria can now produce insulin.

pure human insulin

● **Figure 4.8** Producing human insulin from genetically engineered bacteria.

producing transgenic plants is the **Ti plasmid** of the bacterium *Agrobacterium tumefaciens*, which does insert DNA into the host genome. An example of genetic engineering using this vector is described in the next section.

Genetic engineering in agriculture

More than 60 plant species have so far been genetically engineered, and several thousand field trials of transgenic plants have taken place, mostly in developed countries. So far, commercially valuable crops such as cotton, tobacco, oilseed rape, maize, potatoes and tomatoes have been the subject of most genetic engineering. The traits engineered into the crops show a marked bias towards reducing crop losses caused by pests and diseases. In the year 1993–94, field trials of genetically engineered crops in developed countries were made up approximately as follows:

36% tolerance to herbicides;
32% resistance to insect pests;
14% resistance to viral disease;
14% improvements in crop quality.

The remaining 4% of field trials had other aims, ranging from the production of vaccines and plastics in plants, to changing the colour of cotton.

Let us look at three examples of genetic engineering of crop plants in more detail.

Herbicide tolerance

The herbicide Basta (marketed as Challenge in the United Kingdom) is used in more than 40 countries around the world. Its popularity comes from its ability to kill almost any weed. It also kills crop plants and so must be used before crops grow.

During photosynthesis chloroplasts produce ammonia. The plant disposes of this toxic by-product by means of an enzyme, glutamine synthetase, which combines glutamate and ammonia to give harmless glutamine:

$$\text{ammonia} + \text{glutamate} \xrightarrow{\text{glutamine synthetase}} \text{glutamine}$$

Basta's active ingredient, phosphinothricine, resembles glutamate and binds to the enzyme, blocking

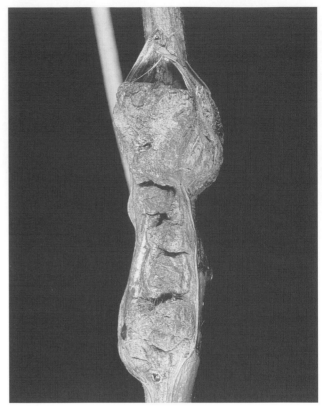

● *Figure 4.9* Tumour (gall) on loganberry stem induced by *Agrobacterium tumefaciens.*

its active site. Ammonia accumulates in the chloroplasts and destroys them, so the plant dies.

A gene from a soil bacterium codes for another enzyme, phosphinothricine acetyl transferase (PAT), which inactivates Basta. The DNA coding for this enzyme has been isolated and, using the bacterium *A. tumefaciens*, can be inserted into the chromosomes of crop plants (including sugar beet, tobacco and oilseed rape) so that they have resistance to Basta.

A. tumefaciens infects wounds in plants and causes the production of a tumour (*figure 4.9*). The bacterium's ability to stimulate tumour production depends on a large plasmid, the Ti plasmid, which carries a group of T (for toxin) genes. When the bacterium invades a plant cell, a copy of the T genes is added to one of the chromosomes of the host. If the wanted gene is inserted into the Ti plasmid before the bacterium invades the plant cell, it is also added into the plant genome (*figure 4.10*). The plant cells, in the form of a callus (page 29), are engineered using the Ti plasmid, and then cultured to produce whole plants.

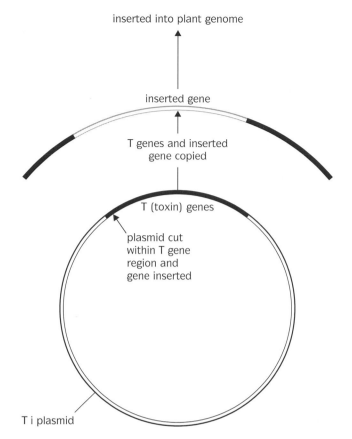

inserted into plant genome

inserted gene

T genes and inserted gene copied

T (toxin) genes

plasmid cut within T gene region and gene inserted

T i plasmid

● **Figure 4.10** Ti plasmid as gene vector.

This method is very effective because it produces crop plants which carry and express the PAT gene in all tissues. Gamete cells also contain the gene, so it is passed on to the plant's offspring.

SAQ 4.3

In 1994 the EU approved a genetically modified tobacco for use as a commercial crop. The tobacco plants contain a bacterial gene for resistance to the herbicide bromoxynil. Permission to market cigarettes made from the tobacco will not be sought until the crop has been grown and tested for five years.

a Explain the value of growing bromoxylin-resistant tobacco plants.

b Suggest what tests might be carried out on the tobacco before cigarettes made from it are marketed.

Plants that repel insects

Another important agricultural development is that of transgenic plants engineered against insect attack. There are a number of examples, including the following.

■ Maize has been protected against the European corn-borer, which eats the leaves of the plant and then burrows into the stalk, eating its way upwards until the plant cannot support the ear. A gene for a toxin which is lethal to insects, but harmless to other animals, has been taken from a bacterium, *Bacillus thuringiensis* (see page 36). Different strains of *B. thuringiensis* produce different toxins. Another is being used to protect leguminous plants from weevils.

■ Potato plants have been protected against insects by incorporation of the pea lectin gene. Lectin is a protein which interferes with digestion in insects, preventing them from absorbing vital substances. It is one of many so-called 'antifeedants' produced by wild plants which are now being transferred to crop plants or from one crop plant to another.

Quality improvement: the 'Flavr Savr' tomato

One of the most publicised uses of genetic engineering in agriculture is the 'Flavr Savr' tomato. Shop-bought tomatoes are often hard and flavourless, because they have been picked whilst green and firm enough to withstand mechanical handling and transport over long distances. They are then ripened by treatment with ethene. This produces red tomatoes, but the flavour is not as good as if the tomatoes had been left to ripen on the plant.

As tomatoes age, they soften. This is caused by the enzyme polygalacturonase, which breaks down cell walls. Production of polygalacturonase in the Flavr Savr tomato has been blocked by the introduction of an **antisense gene**.

Only one strand of the DNA of a gene (the sense strand) is normally transcribed. The complementary strand is the antisense strand. By forcing transcription from the antisense strand an mRNA is produced which is complementary to the mRNA transcribed from the normal gene. The two mRNAs bind together so that no translation can occur, and polygalacturonase production is blocked (*figure 4.11*).

Flavr Savr tomatoes went on sale in the USA in 1994. In January 1995, tomato paste made from

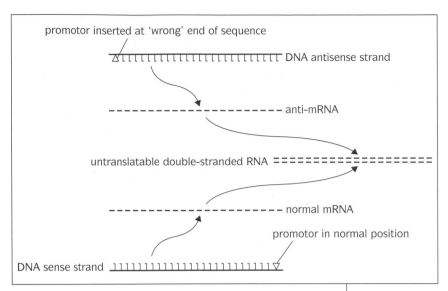

promotor inserted at 'wrong' end of sequence

DNA antisense strand

anti-mRNA

untranslatable double-stranded RNA

normal mRNA

promotor in normal position

DNA sense strand

● **Figure 4.11** The Flavr Savr antisense gene.

these genetically engineered tomatoes was declared safe for human consumption in the UK. Oil from genetically engineered oilseed rape was also declared safe. The two foods became the first two so-called 'whole foods' made by genetic engineering to be given safety clearance in Europe. (Earlier clearances involved organisms used in food production which did not themselves form part of the final food product.)

Watch out for reports of future developments in transgenic crop plants such as the prevention of browning of cut fruit and vegetables, fungus resistance, the production of experimental vaccines in tobacco plants, and the production of biodegradable plastics by plants such as thale cress.

Genetically engineered livestock

In comparison with plants, there are relatively few examples of genetically engineered animals in agricultural use. One example results from looking for ways to prevent cows from developing mastitis, a bacterial infection of the udder. This disease is not only painful for cows, but is also responsible for serious milk losses for the dairy farmer.

In 1991, the government of the Netherlands gave permission for a human gene for lactoferrin to be inserted into fertilised cattle eggs. Lactoferrin is a protein, produced by mammals, that improves resistance to the bacteria that cause mastitis. Cows produce lactoferrin for only a short period when lactating, and it is hoped that cows with the added human gene will produce lactoferrin for much longer. The implantation experiment resulted in one successfully engineered bull, named Herman. In 1992, permission was given to breed from Herman in the hope that he would pass the gene to his daughters, who might then be less susceptible to mastitis.

Some genetically engineered animals are farmed for the products of their inserted genes, usually proteins needed for the treatment of human disease. Typically, the desired gene is combined with a gene coding for a milk protein that is expressed only in the mammary glands. The combined genes are then inserted into fertilised eggs. These are implanted into recipient females. The desired protein can then be harvested from a successfully engineered female's milk. The inserted gene is passed on to any offspring, so that successfully engineered animals of both sexes can be bred to increase the stock of modified animals. The human gene for the protein α_1 antitrypsin, which is required to treat the lung disease hereditary emphysema, has been inserted into sheep. This protein is expensive to produce in the laboratory, but significantly cheaper when extracted from the milk of genetically modified ewes. Similarly, the gene for human clotting factor IX, for treating haemophilia B, has been introduced into sheep.

SAQ 4.4

Explain:

a why it is necessary, in producing a genetically engineered animal, to combine a gene whose product is to be harvested from milk with a gene coding for a milk protein;

b why a gene inserted into a fertilised egg will be passed to that animal's offspring;

c how a successfully engineered male could be identified for breeding.

Benefits and hazards of genetic engineering

We can now create genetically modified organisms for specific uses. In the past, such organisms were derived from selective breeding or arose by chance mutation. In contrast to organisms produced by selective breeding, there is a tendency to see genetically engineered organisms as unnatural and intrinsically unsafe.

As a result of genetic engineering, microorganisms now produce many substances that they would not normally produce. Most of these modified microorganisms are kept in industrial fermenters. Provided that proper containment precautions are used, they cannot affect the general environment. In many cases the strain of organism used, for instance of *E. coli*, survives very poorly in the general environment. The obvious danger is a breakdown of containment, and regulations exist to help prevent contact between such microorganisms and the outside environment. (There is more about the use of microorganisms in genetic engineering, and their containment, in *Microorganisms and Biotechnology*.)

SAQ 4.5

Explain the potential dangers of contact between genetically modified microorganisms and the outside environment.

A totally different set of problems emerges when genetically engineered organisms, such as crop plants and organisms for the biological control of pests, are intended for use in the general environment. Can such organisms be used safely?

The United Kingdom has a good reputation for rigorous consideration of the risks and benefits of releasing genetically modified organisms. Anyone wishing to conduct a field trial must assess the risk to the environment. The Department of Environment then decides, after taking advice from the Advisory Committee on Releases to the Environment (ACRE), whether to issue consent. The approval process is meant to take no longer than 90 days. This procedure has sometimes been seen as a disadvantage for researchers in this country in comparison with Japan and the USA where approval is given in a shorter time. However, a so-called 'fast track' procedure has been allowed in the UK since 1993 for experiments thought to be less hazardous. Much less information needs to be given about these experiments and permission to perform the trial can be given in 30 days. A low-hazard release might be a species that has no natural relatives in the UK and has been modified with a well-known gene, whilst a high-risk release might be a native weed with a gene that had not been transferred before. 'Fast-tracking' has raised many concerns, not least because 30 days is a short time for any opponents of the release to express their fears and have them acted upon.

Consider a field trial that sparked a blaze of publicity in 1994. David Bishop and his colleagues at Oxford sought permission to release genetically modified viruses onto cabbages to test their effect on the caterpillars of the cabbage looper moth. The virus, a baculovirus, had been discovered in a moth that is not native to the UK, the alfalfa looper. The virus had been modified by adding a gene coding for one of the proteins of scorpion venom, which is lethal to insects, but harmless to other animals. An earlier field trial had shown that unmodified virus killed the caterpillars, but that modified virus killed them more quickly, reducing damage to cabbages *(table 4.2)*. The chance of the virus spreading was also reduced, since the modified virus killed caterpillars so rapidly that they produced very few viruses. The new field trial was to measure the effect of the virus on caterpillars of six other moths, and to see how long the virus survived in the soil and on the cabbages. The cabbages were grown in fine netting enclosures to keep out birds and other animals that might spread the virus. Traps prevented insects from getting in.

The opponents of the trial feared that the virus might escape and harm other species of moth, particularly since the field experiment was sited close to the University of Oxford's nature reserve, Wytham Wood. Another potential hazard is that the virus might swap (recombine) genes with other viruses. This is theoretically possible if two

Treatment of cabbage plants	Mean leaf area per cabbage plant eaten by caterpillars/cm²
untreated (control)	107
sprayed with unmodified virus:	
low dose (10^6 virus particles per m²)	100
high dose (10^7–10^8 virus particles per m²)	63
sprayed with genetically modified virus:	
low dose	70
high dose	50

● **Table 4.2** Effect on damage to cabbage plants by looper caterpillars treated with genetically modified and unmodified virus.

different viruses infect the same insect at the same time.

In an attempt to allay fears over the safety of the 1994 trials, the preliminary results were, most unusually, given to a public meeting in November 1994. These results showed that non-target species were much less susceptible to the virus than were the cabbage looper caterpillars. Of the target caterpillars, 80% died after 8 days, in comparison with 1% of non-target species. The results also showed that the genetically engineered virus is some way from being marketed as a biopesticide, since although it kills caterpillars faster than the unmodified virus, the caterpillars still have time to eat holes in the cabbage leaves. Tests will take place for a further five years on the same site, but it will not be possible to test all species of British moths and butterflies.

The aim of this work is to produce a viral insecticide that kills only a specific pest, replacing chemical insecticides that kill a range of organisms and may also damage other organisms. Unmodified viruses have been successfully used in other countries to control particular insects for some time.

SAQ 4.6

Examine *table 4.2* and compare the effects, on damage to cabbage plants by looper caterpillars, of treatment with genetically modified and unmodified viruses.

Consider another experiment, relevant to the Basta-resistant plants described earlier. The

concerns about such genetically engineered crops are that:

■ the modified crop plants will become agricultural weeds or invade natural habitats;

■ the introduced gene(s) will be transferred by pollen to wild relatives whose hybrid offspring will become more invasive;

■ the modified plants will be a direct hazard to humans, domestic animals or other beneficial animals, by being toxic or producing allergies;

■ the herbicide that can now be used on the crop will itself leave toxic residues in the crop.

The results of an investigation to compare invasiveness of normal and genetically modified oilseed rape plants was published by M. Crawley and colleagues at Silwood Park (Imperial College, UK) in 1993. Three genetic lines were compared: non-engineered oilseed rape and two different genetically engineered versions of the same cultivar. The rates of population increase were compared in plants grown in a total of 12 different environments. In each of these, various treatments were applied, including cultivated and uncultivated background vegetation, and presence and absence of various herbivores and pathogens. There was no evidence that genetic engineering increased the invasiveness of these plants. Where differences between them existed, the genetically engineered plants were slightly less invasive than the unmodified plants.

In an attempt to assess the risk of introduced genes being spread from genetically engineered bacteria to wild strains, the Agricultural and Food Research Council investigated the interaction of different strains of *Rhizobium* in field conditions. A strain of *R. leguminosum* whose cells contain a plasmid that can be transferred to other bacteria was used. The plasmid was 'marked' by inserting a gene for antibiotic resistance into it. Large numbers of samples of bacteria over a two-year period revealed that the genetically engineered strain remained in the field soil, but there was no evidence of transfer of the marked plasmid to naturally occurring *Rhizobium*.

Crop plants which contain the toxin genes from *Bacillus thuringiensis* produce their own insecticides. However, a small number of insect populations have evolved resistance to these toxins. The danger is that large numbers of crop plants containing the genes may simply accelerate the evolution of resistance to the toxins.

Safety concerns about the Flavr Savr tomato come not from its antisense gene, but because it also contains a bacterial gene coding for a protein that gives resistance to two antibiotics, kanamycin and neomycin. This gene was inserted so that researchers could identify whether the antisense gene had been taken up. During testing, exposure to kanamycin kills any plant cells that are not transgenic. The United States Food and Drug Administration found no evidence that the protein giving antibiotic resistance would poison consumers or trigger allergies, nor that it would interfere when people took antibiotics. It declared the tomatoes "as safe as tomatoes bred by conventional means". However, there remains a risk that the gene might be transferred to other bacteria, adding to the problem of antibiotic-resistant disease.

Ethical implications of genetic engineering

Ethics are sets of standards by which a particular group of people agree to regulate their behaviour, distinguishing an acceptable from an unacceptable activity. Ethics change with time, because people alter their views according to their knowledge and experience.

In 1974, genetic engineers worldwide accepted a self-imposed ban on some recombinant DNA experiments on the basis that they were too risky. Four years later, their general view was that the risks had been greatly over-estimated. Nevertheless, genetic engineering is a relatively new development, experience of it is limited and a large number of people know virtually nothing about it. Also, development of the techniques has

been rapid. The public was introduced to its first genetically engineered animal in 1982 *(figure 4.12)* and now transgenic animals are standard tools in research and in the production of pharmaceuticals.

An EU committee set up to investigate ethical aspects of biotechnology has as one of its aims that of improving public understanding and acceptance. A survey published in 1993 by the Open University found that four out of five people do not trust industry to tell the truth about genetic engineering and two out of three felt that industry takes short-cuts with safety.

Discuss with your friends whether:

- genetic engineering is in principle acceptable, and if so, in what circumstances;
- it is acceptable to patent a genetically engineered organism or to patent a gene sequence;
- it is acceptable to engineer any organism to produce a product useful to humans;
- it is acceptable to engineer animals to show human diseases for research into those diseases;
- genetically engineered food is acceptable;
- products on sale are adequately labelled to indicate that genetic engineering was involved in their production.

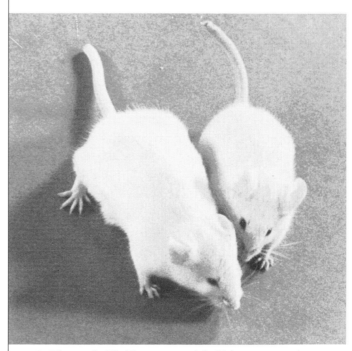

● *Figure 4.12* 'Supermouse' (left) is a transgenic mouse with a rat growth hormone gene. It is almost twice the mass of its normal brother (right).

SUMMARY

■ Genetic engineering involves finding the wanted gene, cloning it and then inserting it into a host organism.

■ The wanted gene may be built up, nucleotide by nucleotide, if its sequence is known. It may be produced by copying mRNA into cDNA. It may be removed from the genome by the use of a restriction enzyme.

■ Restriction enzymes come from bacteria, and defend bacteria against invading viruses. Each enzyme cuts DNA at a specific base sequence of 4–6 bases. The restriction enzymes that are of most use in genetic engineering cut the two strands of DNA in different places. This produces DNA with single strands of nucleotides at each end known as sticky ends. Sticky ends may also be produced by adding strands of single nucleotides to the ends of DNA molecules.

■ Recombinant DNA is made of DNA from two sources. Typically, the same restriction enzyme is used to cut both types of DNA to produce complementary sticky ends. When the two types of DNA are mixed, complementary sticky ends join. 'Nicks' in the sugar–phosphate backbones of the DNA strands are joined by the enzyme DNA ligase.

■ In order to clone a wanted gene, it is inserted into vector DNA. This is often a bacterial plasmid.

■ Recombinant plasmids containing the fragments of a genome, produced by restriction enzymes, are taken up by bacteria, in the presence of Ca^{2+} ions. Bacteria containing the gene required can be identified and cultured. This provides many copies of the gene.

■ Genes are commonly added to plant cells via the Ti plasmid of *Agrobacterium tumefaciens* and to animal cells by using liposomes or viral vectors. DNA may also be inserted into cells by microinjection, electroporation, or by using microprojectiles.

■ Genetic engineering may be beneficial, but may have associated hazards.

Questions

1 Outline the use of restriction enzymes in
   a removing a section of the genome and
   b the formation of recombinant DNA.

2 Describe how *named* organisms can be modified by genetic engineering.

3 Describe one use of genetic engineering in agriculture.

4 Discuss the social and ethical implications of genetic engineering.

5 Discuss the possible benefits and hazards of genetic engineering.

Chapter five

Human genetics

By the end of this chapter you should be able to:

1 describe cystic fibrosis, Huntington's disease and Down's syndrome in humans, and explain how they are inherited;

2 describe how genetic screening is carried out;

3 discuss the advantages and disadvantages of genetic screening and the need for genetic counselling;

4 explain the theoretical basis of gene therapy and discuss its possible benefits and hazards;

5 explain the theoretical basis of genetic fingerprinting and outline how it is carried out;

6 explain the significance of genetic compatibility in transplant surgery, with reference to ABO blood groups and the major histocompatibility (HLA) system.

Since the discovery, in the 1950s and 1960s, of the structure of DNA and the way in which it codes for protein synthesis, very rapid progress has been made in the field of human genetics. An international research programme, the Human Genome Project, has been established with the aim of mapping the location of all the genes on the human chromosomes and determining the precise sequence of human DNA. Already, a number of genes and chromosome abnormalities which cause, or contribute to human disorders have been identified. When an allele of a gene that causes a disorder is discovered, the possibility then exists of identifying carriers of the abnormal allele and advising them of their chances of passing on the disorder to their children. Some disorders result from an interplay of genetic and environmental factors. When genes that contribute to a particular disorder are discovered, people susceptible to that disorder can be identified, perhaps allowing then to alter their lifestyles to help avoid illness. In some cases it may be possible to treat an individual with a genetic disorder by inserting the 'normal' allele of the gene in question, using the techniques of genetic engineering. Individuals may also be identified by analysis of their DNA. Many of these advances in human genetics are to be welcomed, but they also raise ethical and moral issues which need to be debated.

Genetic disorders in humans

A genetic disorder is an inherited malfunction. It may be defined as a disorder that is caused by a genotype that gives rise to a poorly adapted phenotype in an environment in which other genotypes give rise to healthy phenotypes. Remember that both genotype and environment affect the phenotype. In *Central Concepts in Biology* you met an example of a genetic disorder: sickle cell anaemia. This results from the inheritance of the recessive allele, H^S, of the gene for the β polypeptide of haemoglobin. The homozygote recessive, H^SH^S, has sickle cell anaemia, whilst the homozygote dominant, H^NH^N, is healthy. The heterozygote, H^NH^S, only shows symptoms of disease in extreme conditions, such as when exercising at high altitude, when the oxygen concentration in the blood may become very low.

Genetic disorders may be caused by the inheritance of:

■ gene mutations, either on a sex chromosome or on an autosome (a chromosome that is *not* a sex chromosome);
■ changes in chromosome structure;
■ changes in the number of chromosomes.

An example of an sex-linked disorder, haemophilia, is described in *Central Concepts in Biology*. The gene concerned is found on the X chromosome. The locations of some of the other loci on the X chromosome that are known to be involved in disease are shown in *figure 5.1*.

Cystic fibrosis

Cystic fibrosis is an example of a disorder caused by a mutation on an autosome. It is the most

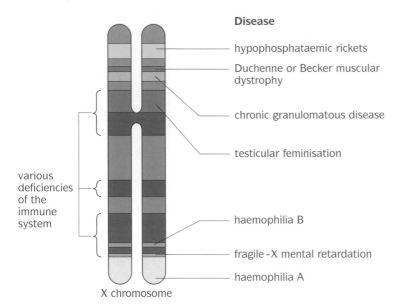

Disease	Brief description of disease
hypophosphataemic rickets	kidneys fail to retain phosphate, leading to rickets
Duchenne or Becker muscular dystrophy	progressive muscular weakness, wheelchair by age 10, death commonly by age 20. Some mentally retarded. Becker muscular dystrophy is less severe.
chronic granulomatous disease	white blood cells unable to kill bacteria, leading to recurrent infections and death in childhood
testicular feminisation	poor development of testes
haemophilia B	faulty factor IX protein which is needed for blood clotting
fragile-X mental retardation	mental retardation
haemophilia A	faulty factor VIII protein which is needed for blood clotting

● *Figure 5.1* Locations of some of the genes on the human X chromosome, which are involved in known diseases.

common major genetic disease among white people, affecting about 1 in 2500 babies.

In cystic fibrosis, the transport of chloride ions and water by the cells lining the airways and gut is disrupted. This causes thick, dehydrated mucus to build up in the lungs, making it easy for harmful bacterial infections to occur. Recurrent infections scar the lungs and eventually lead to lung failure. Frequent physiotherapy is necessary to clear mucus from the lungs. The mucus also blocks the secretion of digestive enzymes from the pancreas into the duodenum. Enzymes are given in tablet form to improve digestion. Before 1940, more than 80% of affected children died before the age of five. Improved treatments now mean that the average life expectancy is about 30 years.

Cystic fibrosis is caused by a recessive allele of a gene locus on the long arm of chromosome 7. (The human chromosomes are shown in *figure 5.3*.) Homozygote recessives show the disease; heterozygotes are carriers (between 1 in 20 and 1 in 25 individuals in white races). Two carrier parents have a 1 in 4 chance at each conception of producing an offspring with cystic fibrosis.

The gene was identified in 1989. The 'normal' allele codes for a protein that forms an ion channel in the cell surface membrane of cells of the airways, lung and gut. The channel allows chloride ions to move out of the cells. This movement carries water with it which keeps the surface of the lungs wet and clean. One mutation of the gene, which accounts for about 70% of the cases of cystic fibrosis, results in the loss of one amino acid about one-third of the way along the protein molecule. This disrupts a binding site for ATP and interferes with the normal functioning of the ion channel. Another 15% of the cases are caused by one of three different changes to the ion channel. The remaining cases are caused by rare mutations. Over 100 defects of the ion channel gene have been identified. This has important implications for both genetic screening and gene therapy, as will be seen later.

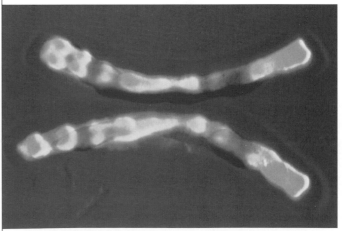

● *Figure 5.2* Light micrograph of a pair of human chromosomes I showing banding pattern (× 15 000).

Until recently, cystic fibrosis was known only in humans, and the lack of a suitable animal model on which to test new drugs and treatments hindered the search for a cure. Now, strains of laboratory mice have been created, by genetic engineering, that suffer symptoms similar to those shown in the human disease. However, for many people this is not an ethically acceptable use of animals.

Huntington's disease (chorea)

Huntington's disease is an example of a disorder resulting from a change in chromosome structure. It is a neurological disorder resulting in involuntary muscle movement (chorea) and progressive mental deterioration. Brain cells are lost and the ventricles of the brain become much larger. The age of onset is variable, but occurs most commonly in middle age, so that sufferers may have children before they know that they themselves have the disease.

The gene was identified in 1993 and lies near the end of the short arm of chromosome 4. The mutation is inherited as a dominant allele. Sufferers are heterozygotes and have a 1 in 2 chance of passing on the condition. The mutation is an unstable segment of a gene coding for a protein now called 'huntingtin'. In people who do not show the disease, the segment is made up of between 11 and 34 repeats of the triplet of bases, C–A–G (cytosine–adenine–guanine). Individuals with the disease have between 42 and 100 repetitions of the C–A–G triplet. This is referred to as a 'stutter' in the gene. Similar 'stuttering' triplets are the cause of other genetic diseases such as fragile X syndrome and myotonic dystrophy.

In Huntington's disease there is a rough inverse correlation between the number of times the triplet of bases is repeated and the age of onset of the disease: the more copies of the triplet, the earlier the disease appears. One of the longest repeating sequences (86 triplets) found came from a child in an extended family in Venezuela, who showed symptoms of the disease at the age of two years.

Down's syndrome

Down's syndrome is a disorder caused most commonly by a change in chromosome number, but may result from a change in chromosome structure. It occurs in 1 in 700 births, but the frequency increases with parental age. A person with Down's syndrome has characteristic folds on the eyelids (epicanthal folds) and a slightly flattened face. Heart defects are common, muscle tone poor and stature short. There is a degree of mental retardation, but this varies from very mild to severe. Down's syndrome children are usually very affectionate and happy. Life expectancy used to be poor because of heart defects and infections, but is now considerably improved.

Down's syndrome is caused by having an extra copy of the genes on the long arm of chromosome 21. This can occur in two ways: by having an extra chromosome 21 (**trisomy 21**) or by a **translocation** (a structural mutation of a chromosome in which a portion of one chromosome is transferred to another). Only about 5% of the cases of Down's syndrome are caused by translocation.

Trisomy 21

Figure 5.3 shows a karyotype of an individual with Down's syndrome, showing three examples of chromosome 21 (see also *box 5B*, page 59). Trisomies result from errors in cell division. The

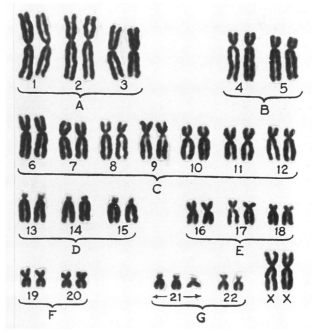

● **Figure 5.3** Karyotype of a human female with Down's syndrome (trisomy 21). The chromosomes are arranged in groups (A–G) according to their structure.

most common cause is a failure of homologous chromosomes to separate during meiosis I. This is called **nondisjunction**, and results in one daughter cell having both members of a chromosome pair. When this cell is fertilised by a gamete carrying the normal haploid number of chromosomes, the resulting zygote will have three examples of one chromosome, rather than the normal two. This can occur for any chromosome. However, most trisomies are lethal and so are seen for only a few autosomes and for the sex chromosomes. Meiotic nondisjunction resulting in trisomy 21 is shown in *figure 5.4*. This is the usual origin of about 95% of the cases of Down's syndrome.

Most cases of trisomy 21 arise by chance, so that this form of Down's syndrome is not inherited. But the likelihood of the chance mistake occurring increases with parental age. In about 75% of the cases of this type of Down's syndrome the extra chromosome has come from the mother, with mothers over the age of 35 years particularly at risk *(figure 5.5)*. In a mature woman, oocytes have been held in the ovary in an enormously extended prophase I of meiosis from before her birth to shortly before ovulation of the oocyte in question. It is likely that the cell is vulnerable to internal and external factors during this long time, resulting in a greater chance of nondisjunction occurring.

Spermatocytes do not undergo an extended meiosis, so that this explanation cannot apply to those cases in which the extra chromosome derives from the father.

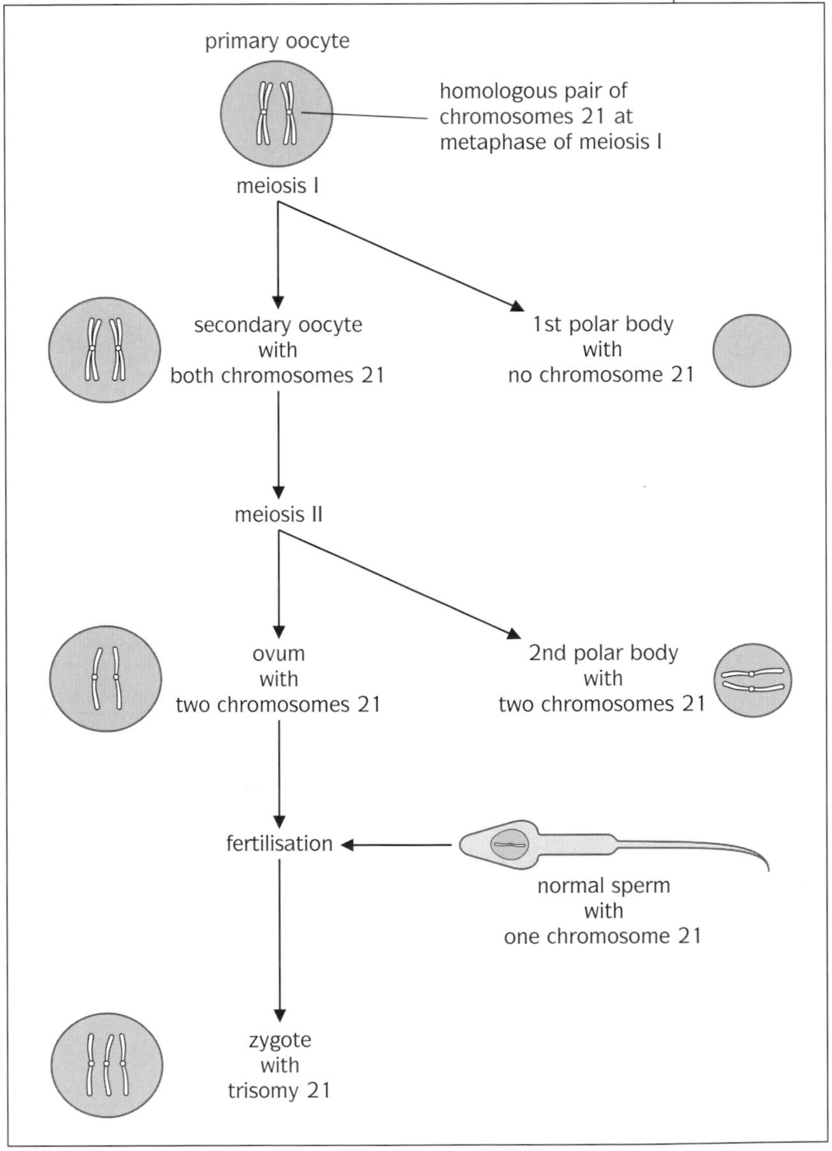

primary oocyte

homologous pair of chromosomes 21 at metaphase of meiosis I

meiosis I

secondary oocyte with both chromosomes 21

1st polar body with no chromosome 21

meiosis II

ovum with two chromosomes 21

2nd polar body with two chromosomes 21

fertilisation

normal sperm with one chromosome 21

zygote with trisomy 21

● **Figure 5.4** Down's syndrome (trisomy 21) caused by meiotic nondisjunction. Only the homologous pair of chromosomes 21 is shown.

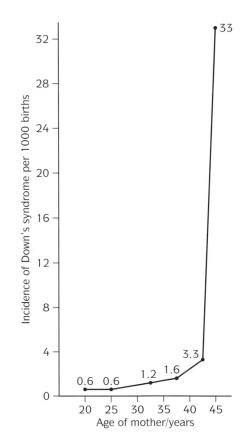

● **Figure 5.5** The relationship between the incidence of Down's syndrome and maternal age.

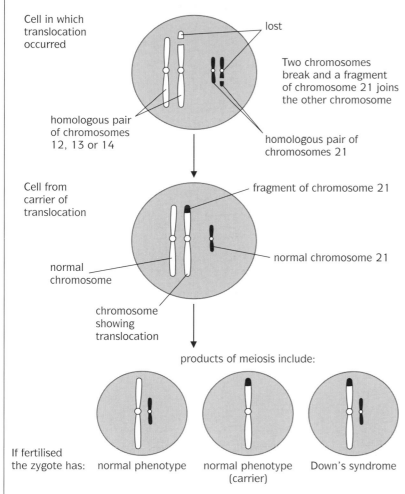

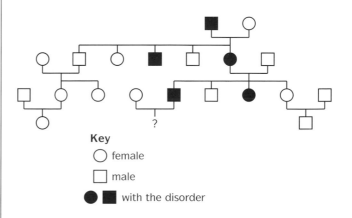

● *Figure 5.6* Down's syndrome caused by chromosome translocation.

Translocation of part of chromosome 21

A translocation involves a chromosome breaking and a portion of it moving to another chromosome. The end of the long arm of chromosome 21 may break off and join onto one of the other autosomes (usually onto chromosomes 13, 14 or 15). After meiosis, a gamete may receive not only a chromosome 21, but also a chromosome with the end of the long arm of chromosome 21 attached to it. This gamete therefore has two examples of the genes at the end of the long arm of chromosome 21. When such a gamete is fertilised by a gamete with the normal haploid complement of chromosomes, the resulting zygote is effectively trisomic for chromosome 21 and the individual shows Down's syndrome *(figure 5.6)*. This form of Down's syndrome can be inherited.

Pedigree analysis

In various circumstances, potential parents may be concerned about the risk they have of producing a child with a particular genetic disorder. Such circumstances might be that they have already produced one child with a genetic disorder or that a particular disorder is known to be present in one or both of their families.

When the condition is caused by an allele of a gene showing a simple inheritance pattern, for instance cystic fibrosis, the probability of being a carrier for, and of passing on, the condition, can be determined by **pedigree analysis**. A **pedigree** is a family tree of a group of related people (a **kindred**). Plainly, if a couple have already produced one child with cystic fibrosis, they must both be carriers and have a 1 in 4 chance of producing another child with the same condition.

SAQ 5.1

Examine *figure 5.7*, which shows the pedigree of a kindred, some of whose members show a rare genetic disorder.

a Decide whether the genetic disorder is caused by a recessive or a dominant mutation.

b Calculate the probability of the individual marked '?' showing the disorder.

● *Figure 5.7* A kindred showing a genetic disorder.

Genetic screening

Pedigree analysis can only determine the *probability* of an individual being a carrier or showing a genetic disorder. Certainty comes from some form of test for the condition or for the genotype that causes it. This is known as genetic screening. There are two applications of such tests: to possible carriers and to a developing embryo.

Genetic screening of carriers

Until recently, few genetic disorders could be detected in carriers. However, once a gene is identified and sequenced, a DNA probe can be made (page 44).

A sample of blood, or cheek cells, is taken from the person being screened, and the DNA probe used to see if their DNA contains the gene concerned. A probe that identifies one mutant allele causing a condition such as cystic fibrosis will not identify a different mutation; several tests may be needed. At the moment, probes have been made for only a small number of genetic disorders.

Genetic screening of an embryo in vitro

After in vitro fertilisation (page 19), a single cell can be removed from the 8-cell stage of a developing embryo *(figure 5.8)* and its DNA tested. Only if the outcome of the test is satisfactory is the embryo put into the uterus.

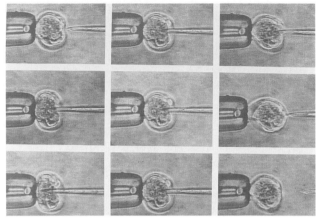

● *Figure 5.8* Photomicrographs of the removal for genetic screening of one cell of an 8-cell human embryo. The photographs are arranged in sequence from left to right. A micropipette enters the embryo from the right and collects a cell (bottom row, left).

Box 5A Amniocentesis

An ultrasound scanner is used to detect the position of the fetus and placenta, and a hypodermic syringe inserted into the amniotic cavity, carefully avoiding placenta and fetus *(figure 5.9a)*. A sample of amniotic fluid is withdrawn. This contains fetal cells which can be cultured and tested in various ways. The technique is usually performed between 13 and 16 weeks of pregnancy and the results are available 2–3 weeks later. There is a slight risk of spontaneous abortion as a result of the test procedure.

Chorionic villus sampling

A fine catheter is inserted via the vagina and cervix into the actively dividing cells of the chorionic villi of the placenta *(figure 5.9b)*. This technique carries a slightly higher risk of inducing spontaneous abortion than amniocentesis, but it can be performed slightly earlier (9–12 weeks) in pregnancy. It also yields results quicker, because the cells taken are already actively dividing. The earlier testing time and the speed of getting results are both important to parents with a high risk of producing a child with a disorder.

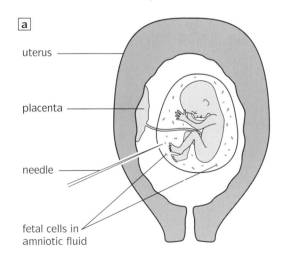

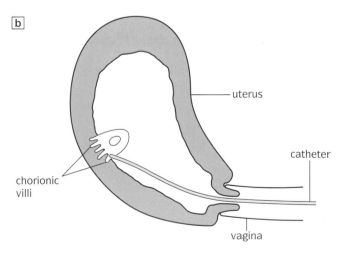

● *Figure 5.9* **a** Amniocentesis, 13–16 weeks of pregnancy. **b** Chorionic villus sampling, 9–12 weeks of pregnancy.

Genetic screening of the fetus in the uterus

It is possible to obtain samples of fetal cells at an early stage of development by **amniocentesis** or by **chorionic villus sampling** *(box 5A and figure 5.9)*. These cells can then be **karyotyped** *(box 5B)* or their DNA extracted and analysed as described before.

Box 5B Karyotype analysis

Chromosomal abnormalities are detected by preparing a karyotype. Cells from a suitable source, such as blood, amniotic fluid or chorionic villi, are cultured and stimulated to undergo mitosis. After 3 days, colchicine is added. This inhibits spindle formation so that the cells are held in metaphase of mitosis. The cells are then induced to take up water by osmosis so that they swell and the chromosomes separate. In this form they can be stained and a photomicrograph taken. The chromosomes are then cut from the photograph and arranged in homologous pairs, as in *figure 5.3*. A gene probe with a fluorescent marker can be applied before the cells are photographed. The cells are then photographed in fluorescent light to reveal the marker *(figure 5.10)*.

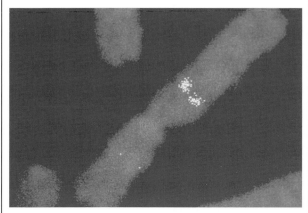

● **Figure 5.10** Photomicrograph of human chromosomes treated with a fluorescent marker (× 15 000).

Genetic counselling

Suppose that a couple has been identified as being at risk of having a child with a genetic disorder. A specially qualified genetic counsellor provides advice, both before and after screening.

Counselling aims to make sure that the parents have a proper understanding of the probability of the risk that they have of producing an affected child. The severity of the disorder concerned is also explained. The options available to the couple are considered in the light of their religious and moral beliefs and their cultural background. The hope is that the couple can then make a decision in an informed manner. The results of any tests and the discussions are confidential, so that a couple has a free choice of what to do next.

Counselling helps potential parents to decide:

■ whether or not to have children;
■ whether, if both are carriers of a recessive mutation, to avoid the risk by having artificial insemination by donor;
■ whether to use in vitro fertilisation and test the embryo before implantation;
■ whether to start a pregnancy, but terminate it if prenatal screening shows that the embryo is affected;
■ whether to avoid the risk by accepting gamete or embryo donation.

Genetic screening raises a number of problematical issues, which you should think about and discuss with your friends.

■ Who should be screened?
■ What would be the advantages and disadvantages of screening everyone for one or more inherited disorders, assuming that this were financially possible?
■ Who should have access to information derived from screening?
■ Do parents have the right to terminate the pregnancy of a fetus with a genetic disorder?
■ Should an individual who is found to be a carrier of an inherited disorder tell other members of the family who might also be affected?

Gene therapy

Gene therapy involves treating genetic disease by altering a patient's natural genotype. There are two potential approaches to such therapy:

■ **germ cell** therapy of sperm, egg or early embryo;
■ **somatic cell** (body cell) therapy.

These are distinguished in *figure 5.11*. Germ cell therapy, although technically possible, is not an

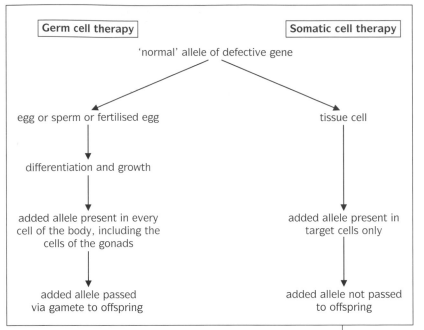

Germ cell therapy	Somatic cell therapy

'normal' allele of defective gene

egg or sperm or fertilised egg → differentiation and growth → added allele present in every cell of the body, including the cells of the gonads → added allele passed via gamete to offspring

tissue cell → added allele present in target cells only → added allele not passed to offspring

● *Figure 5.11* Germ cell versus somatic cell gene therapy.

ethically acceptable option for the foreseeable future, since inserted genes would be passed from generation to generation with unknown, and possibly damaging, effects in any offspring.

Theoretically there are three possible ways of altering the genotype:

■ repair of the gene responsible for the disease;
■ replacement of the defective gene by a normal one;
■ addition of a normal gene, leaving the defective one in position.

Only the last approach provides a feasible method once a zygote has started to divide and develop. However, it can work only when the disorder is the result of a recessive allele of a gene.

SAQ 5.2

Explain why the addition to a cell of a normal gene, leaving the defective one in position, can work only when the disorder results from a recessive allele of a gene.

In some therapies, cells are removed from the body, the therapeutic gene inserted into them, and the cells replaced. In these circumstances any of the methods of delivering DNA into a cell may be used (page 44). In other therapies the DNA is put

into the tissue concerned without the need to remove cells from the body. DNA may be inserted into tissue cells by use of a viral vector or by a nonviral delivery system such as a liposome.

The first successful gene therapy was performed in 1990 on a four-year-old girl from Cleveland, Ohio. She suffered from the very rare genetic disorder known as severe combined immune deficiency (SCID). In this disorder, the immune system is crippled and sufferers die in infancy from common infections. Attempts have been made with some children showing the condition to isolate them from bacteria and viruses inside plastic 'bubbles'.

The defect in SCID involves an inability to make an enzyme, adenosine deaminase (ADA), which is vital for the functioning of the immune system. Some of the child's white blood cells (T lymphocytes) were removed, and normal copies of the ADA gene introduced into them, using a virus as vector. The cells were then replaced. This is not a permanent cure. Regular transfusions (every three to five months) of genetically engineered white cells are necessary to keep the immune system functioning. After treatment, the girl now attends normal school, and has had no more than the average number of infections.

Two gene therapies were begun in 1993 in the United Kingdom: for SCID and for cystic fibrosis. In the latter, nine adult males received therapy, and three received a placebo in a 'double-blind' trial *(box 5C)*. Copies of the normal allele of the gene

Box 5C

In a **double-blind trial** of a new drug, vaccine or other therapy, neither patients nor doctors know who is taking the new therapy and who is taking a neutral, inert substance known as a **placebo**. Such a trial aims to avoid any bias that might arise because patients 'expect' to get better as a result of taking the therapy. Doctors might also report their patients' condition differently according to their belief in the therapy. Organisers of the trial therefore allocate patients to actual treatment or to treatment with a placebo in a randomised way, unknown to the doctors.

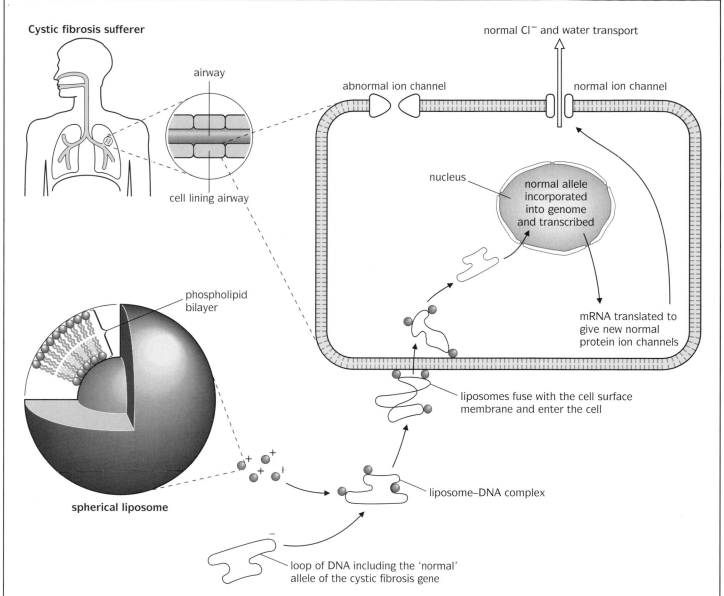

Cystic fibrosis sufferer

airway

normal Cl⁻ and water transport

abnormal ion channel

normal ion channel

cell lining airway

nucleus

normal allele incorporated into genome and transcribed

phospholipid bilayer

mRNA translated to give new normal protein ion channels

liposomes fuse with the cell surface membrane and enter the cell

spherical liposome

liposome–DNA complex

loop of DNA including the 'normal' allele of the cystic fibrosis gene

● *Figure 5.12* Gene therapy for cystic fibrosis.

for cystic fibrosis were inserted into loops of DNA which were then attached to liposomes. Positively charged liposomes attract negatively charged DNA and form a complex with it. The liposome–DNA complexes were then sprayed as an aerosol of fine droplets into the noses of the recipient patients. An earlier American trial of a potential therapy for cystic fibrosis used viruses as vectors, but these set up reactions in already badly damaged lungs. Liposomes were thought to be a less harmful vector. The therapy is shown diagramatically in *figure 5.12*.

It is thought that only a small percentage of cells of the airways (< 10%) need to express the inserted gene to avoid the effects of cystic fibrosis.

However, this therapy cannot provide a permanent cure for cystic fibrosis, since cells from the airways are shed constantly. Male patients were chosen for this trial to avoid the risks of the gene being passed on to any children, since virtually all men with cystic fibrosis are sterile.

The results of the trials were reported in January 1995. The effectiveness of the treatment was determined by measuring the potential difference across the layer of cells lining the nose. Because of their defective ion channels, this potential difference is higher in cystic fibrosis sufferers than in healthy people. The trial showed that treatment with liposome–DNA complexes reduced the potential difference by about 20%, suggesting that some normal ion channels were produced by the cells lining the nose. The effect lasted for about a week. This is not good enough for the procedure to be recommended as a treatment in its present form, but is an encouraging result for its further development. None of the volunteers suffered any unpleasant side-effects from the treatment and the next step is to spray the liposome–DNA complexes into the lungs.

The possible benefits and hazards of gene therapy

There are more than 4000 known inherited genetic disorders. Many inherited conditions are very difficult or impossible to treat effectively. At best, existing treatment reduces the symptoms of the disorder. Gene therapy may not offer a permanent cure for any of the disorders, but it promises an effective treatment.

However, when any new treatment is introduced into medicine, its benefits must be balanced against any risks associated with the treatment. In the United Kingdom a government committee under the chairmanship of Sir Cecil Clothier reported on the ethics of gene therapy in 1992. A number of issues were considered, including:

■ should somatic cell therapy, germ cell therapy or both be allowed?

■ what type of patient should receive gene therapy first?

■ what type of condition should be changed by therapy?

Agreement was reached that gene therapy should for the moment be confined to somatic cells and to life-threatening conditions for which there is no alternative therapy.

There may be hazards associated with the practicalities of a particular therapy and these must be minimised. When a gene is inserted to replace a defective gene, the treatment should ideally work only where the disease symptoms are shown. If the affected cells cannot specifically be targeted, the new DNA may enter other cells and have unforeseen effects. So far, no serious pathological conditions have occurred as a result of gene transfer.

Genetic fingerprinting (DNA profiling)

Genetic fingerprinting was developed by Professor Alec Jeffreys and his research group at the University of Leicester in 1984. They found that sections of DNA that do not code for part of a gene contain short lengths of highly repetitive sequences of bases (Variable Number Tandem Repeats: VNTRs).

Box 5D Some dates in human genetics

1876 Colour blindness shown to be inherited by J.Horner.

1910 Sickle cell anaemia identified as a disease by J.Herrick.

1911 Colour blindness gene shown by E.B.Wilson to be on the X chromosome.

1949 Sickle cell anaemia shown by L.Pauling to be a defect in the structure of haemoglobin.

1956 Human body cells shown to contain 23 pairs of chromosomes;
Sickle cell anaemia shown by V.Ingram to result from a single change of an amino acid in β globin.

1967 Amniocentesis and chromosome analysis developed.

1981 Cancer-causing genes identified.
Diagnosis of sickle cell trait by analysis of DNA.

1983 Gene for Huntington's disease located to chromosome 4.

1984 Development of genetic fingerprinting by A.Jeffreys.

1985 Cystic fibrosis gene located to chromosome 7.

1986 Muscular dystrophy gene identified.

1987 The Human Genome Project proposed by R.Sinsheimer.

1989 Cystic fibrosis gene identified.
Clothier Committee set up in the United Kingdom to discuss the ethics of gene therapy.

1990 First successful human gene therapy for severe combined immunodeficiency (SCID)in the USA.
Human Genome Project begun.

1991 Gene therapy for haemophilia attempted in China.

1993 Huntington's disease gene identified.
First human gene therapy trial in the United Kingdom approved by the Clothier committee.
Gene therapy for SCID and cystic fibrosis begun in the UK.

The number of repeats, and hence the size of the VNTRs, varies markedly between individuals, and is inherited: half of the repeats derive from the father, half from the mother of the individual concerned. Only identical twins have the same numbers of repeat sequences. A genetic fingerprint is a method of revealing the differences in size of VNTRs of different individuals.

The sequence of events is shown in *figure 5.13*. DNA is first extracted from a cell sample. Restriction enzymes (page 39) are used to cut the DNA. The enzyme used in the United Kingdom is HinfI, and in the United States HaeIII. These cut close to, but not within the VNTR regions and so release them intact. The DNA fragments produced by the restriction enzyme can be separated according to size by agarose gel electrophoresis (*figure 5.14* and *box 5E*). The smaller the fragments, the further they travel towards the anode in the time allowed. The pattern of bands on the gel is invisible at this stage; the next sequence of steps allows it to be made visible.

The DNA fragments are transferred to a nylon membrane by **Southern blotting**. This involves covering the gel with a nylon membrane and then adding a layer of absorbent paper, such as paper

● *Figure 5.14* An agarose gel electrophoresis bath.

towels. The DNA is drawn upwards, onto the nylon membrane, by capillary action. The DNA fragments are denatured, by heating, to give single-stranded DNA. A radioactive (^{32}P) DNA probe with a base sequence complementary to one of the VNTR sequences is used to locate particular bands. The probe then binds with its complementary single-stranded DNA, and any excess probe is washed off.

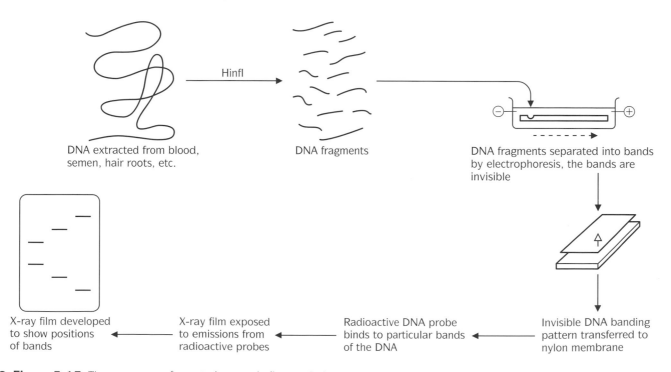

DNA extracted from blood, semen, hair roots, etc.

DNA fragments

DNA fragments separated into bands by electrophoresis, the bands are invisible

X-ray film developed to show positions of bands ← X-ray film exposed to emissions from radioactive probes ← Radioactive DNA probe binds to particular bands of the DNA ← Invisible DNA banding pattern transferred to nylon membrane

● *Figure 5.13* The sequence of events in genetic fingerprinting.

probes are accurately located by
film over the nylon membrane.
m ^{32}P blacken the film, so that the
of DNA profiling is a pattern of dark
stripes on an X-ray film.

x 5E Gel electrophoresis.

DNA that has been cleaved by one or more restriction enzymes is placed in a 'well' at one end of a gel made of agarose (a very pure form of agar) in an electrophoresis bath *(figure 5.14)*. A direct electric current is then passed through the gel and each fragment moves towards the anode at a rate dependent on its mass. This produces a series of bands of DNA which can be revealed by a fluorescent stain *(figure 5.15)*. Each band consists of fragments of DNA of a particular size, which can be worked out by running a control DNA sample from another well in the same gel. The control is a mixture of DNA fragments of known size, referred to as 'markers'. The distance moved by the markers is always the same when a given electric current is applied to a particular gel for the same time, and in the same conditions.

Jeffreys produced two probes which located particular VNTRs that occur in several different places in the human genome. Such probes are called **multi-locus** probes, because the probe binds to the DNA in many places and produces a fingerprint with many bands.

In unrelated persons, only one in four bands may match by chance, so if two samples of DNA produce the same pattern of many bands, it is assumed that they come from the same person.

Comparisons between different patterns can investigate the likelihood that two persons are related, making DNA profiles extremely helpful in determining possible relationship in immigration or paternity disputes *(figure 5.16)*. When making comparisons of DNA a standard control sample of DNA fragments of known sizes is always used.

SAQ 5.3

Examine *figure 5.16*, which shows diagrammatic DNA profiles of a mother, her child and the possible father of the child. Decide whether the possible father is the actual father of the child.

Multi-locus probes are also used forensically, provided a large enough sample of DNA is available.

Single-locus probes bind to DNA at one point only, giving a genetic fingerprint of two bands for an individual, one from the maternal, and one from the paternal chromosome of the homologous pair of chromosomes carrying that VNTR. Single-locus probes are more sensitive than multi-locus probes and can be used to investigate small samples of DNA or even partially decomposed samples of DNA.

In forensic work, several different single-locus probes are used on a single sample. When four different probes are used, as in the United

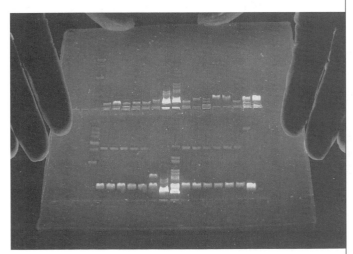

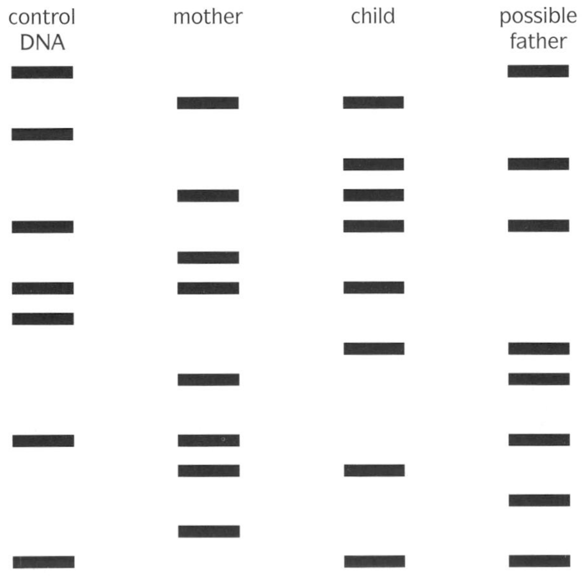

● *Figure 5.15* Agarose gel showing bands of DNA fluorescing in ultraviolet light.

● *Figure 5.16* Diagrammatic DNA profiles of a mother, her child, and the possible father of the child.

Kingdom, the DNA profile has eight different bands *(figure 5.17)*. Using more than one single-locus probe improves the validity of the test.

Samples containing DNA are often available after crimes of violence: for instance, semen after rape. Suppose that when this profile is compared with that of a suspect, any one of the bands is clearly different: the suspect could *not* have been the source of the sample.

Suppose instead that a full match occurs. First, the possibility of a close relative of the suspect having committed the crime must be investigated. If that is eliminated, an estimate must then be made of the likelihood of such a match occurring by chance with an unrelated person (the 'match probability'). Such a calculation is based on the assumption that the banding patterns are distributed randomly in a community. However, the members of some ethnic or religious groups are likely to have partners from within their group. This degree of 'inbreeding' increases the chance that a child will inherit the same VNTR from both parents and be homozygous for that sequence. A genetic fingerprint would show one (dark) band rather than the two expected (lighter) bands. This in turn requires a different calculation of the probability of a match occurring by chance than that which assumes that each person has two different bands.

Problems of this type leave evidence from DNA profiling open to challenge in court, particularly in the United States. In some cases, some questionable statistics have been used because it has been assumed that the frequencies measured in small samples are representative of large populations. The only answer to this problem is to sample the variation of many populations, especially those from different ethnic origins. Unfortunately, there can be misunderstandings by juries of the use of probabilities in connection with DNA profiling.

The second set of problems that have left DNA profiling evidence open to challenge results from variations in technique, which can give variations in results. Until standards are agreed and are enforced, two independent sources of profiles should be used before presenting evidence to a court.

Great care must also be taken to avoid contamination of a DNA sample under test, not only by other DNA but by any other chemical that might affect the action of the restriction enzymes.

There are proposals to set up in the United Kingdom, in April 1995, a database of criminals' DNA profiles. DNA samples will be taken from all suspects arrested for offences punishable by imprisonment. It is hoped that this will help to catch criminals who repeatedly commit offences such as rape. In this context, you should not overlook the value of DNA profiling in establishing innocence.

Uses of DNA profiling other than in human paternity testing and in forensic science include:

- genetic screening;
- identifying animals or plants with particular alleles of a gene for selective breeding;
- identifying the particular strain of a microbial infection or contamination so that the correct treatment can be applied;
- the profiling of populations of animals to prevent unnecessary inbreeding in breeding programmes (e.g. Californian condors, Galapagos tortoises);
- establishing paternity in animal behaviour studies;
- confirming animal pedigrees;

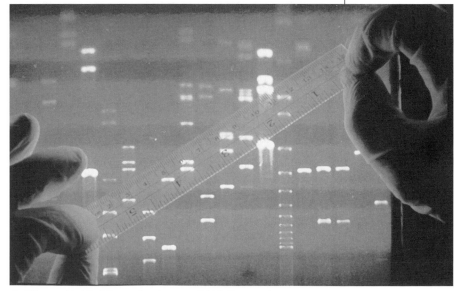

● *Figure 5.17* Measuring human DNA fingerprints.

- monitoring the success of bone marrow transplants;
- establishing genetic diversity for gene banking;
- identifying illegal trading of protected species, such as ivory, rhino horn and whale meat;
- identifying organisms taken from the wild rather than legitimately bred in captivity.

Genetic compatibility in transplant surgery

When tissue from one person, the **donor**, is transplanted into another, the **recipient**, the recipient (unless donor and recipient are identical twins) will produce an *immune response* against the transplanted tissue. The tissue will eventually be destroyed. This is **tissue rejection**. It is based on genetic differences between individuals. The ability to accept the transplanted tissue or **compatibility** depends on the degree of similarity between individuals at particular gene loci.

The immune system recognises self or not-self cells via particular molecules (proteins or glycoproteins) on the cell surface membranes. These molecules act as antigens against which antibodies can be produced. An antibody combines with its specific antigen, triggering the body's defence mechanisms to destroy the cell concerned.

The **ABO blood group locus** and the genes of the **major histocompatibility complex (MHC)** are all-important in transplant surgery. The MHC was first identified in white blood cells and so is also called the **human leucocyte antigen system (HLA)**.

ABO blood groups

The four blood groups A, B, AB and O are characterised by different antigen molecules on the surface of the red blood cells and different antibodies in the blood plasma. These, and the possible genotypes, are shown in *table 5.1*.

An individual of blood group A could not be given blood from a donor of blood group B. The donated red cells carry the B antigen, and the

ABO blood group	Genotypes	Phenotypes	
		Red blood cell antigen	Plasma antibody
O	$I^O I^O$	none	anti-A and anti-B
A	$I^A I^A$ or $I^A I^O$	A	anti-B
B	$I^B I^B$ or $I^B I^O$	B	anti-A
AB	$I^A I^B$	A and B	none

● **Table 5.1** The genotypes and phenotypes of the ABO blood groups.

recipient's plasma contains anti-B plasma antibody. The donated cells would be clumped together by the plasma antibody, with disastrous consequences. Obviously, transplant donor and recipient must 'match' in terms of blood group.

SAQ 5.4

Examine *table 5.1* and explain:

a why
  i individuals of blood group O can donate small volumes of blood to a recipient of any blood group;
  ii individuals of blood group AB can receive small volumes of blood from a donor of any blood group.

b the consequences of giving a large volume of group O blood to a recipient of blood group A.

Major histocompatibility complex (MHC)/human leucocyte antigen (HLA) system

The antigens A and B are confined to the surface of red cells. All other cells, but not red blood cells, carry antigens coded for by the four gene loci of the HLA system.

The four gene loci, called HLA-A, HLA-B, HLA-C and HLA-D, coding for these cell surface antigens are very close together on chromosome 6 of the human genome. Three of the four loci, A, B and C, are tightly linked. The D locus is separated from these by a region containing other genes, but even so is very rarely separated from them by crossing over in prophase of meiosis I. The block of four gene loci, which tends to be inherited as a unit, is called a **haplotype**.

Each of the four loci has a large number of alleles. The very many possible combinations of these account for the differences between individuals in their HLA antigens. The probability of finding a matching donor in the general population for an individual in need of a transplant is very small. However, since the loci are inherited as a haplotype, the chances of finding a suitable donor within an individual's family are much greater. As you can see from *figure 5.18*, a child receives one of the mother's two haplotypes and one of the father's two haplotypes.

SAQ 5.5

Examine *figure 5.18* and calculate the probability of a second child in this family having:

a the same haplotypes as the first;

b fewer than four antigens the same as the first.

Given the number of alleles at the HLA loci, it is fortunate for potential transplant recipients that not all have the same effect. Some of the HLA antigens produce stronger reactions than others. Provided these are matched between donor and recipient a transplant stands a good chance of success.

Genetic engineering has been used by the Cambridgeshire company Imutran to produce pigs which do **not** carry the HLA loci. These pigs carry a human gene for a cell surface membrane protein that prevents attack by one of the body's defence systems. The response of the pigs' hearts to human blood is being tested to see if such pigs could supply material for transplanting into humans.

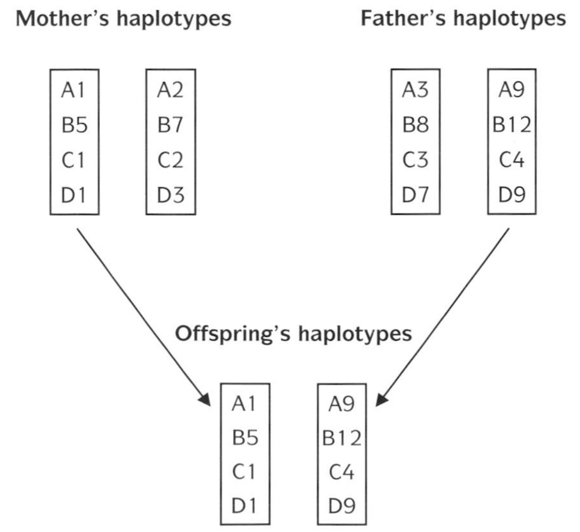

SUMMARY

■ Cystic fibrosis is inherited as a recessive mutation on chromosome 7. There are a number of different mutations. All affect the functioning of a protein ion channel in the cell surface membrane of lung and gut cells, resulting in a build-up of viscous mucus.

■ Huntington's disease is inherited as a dominant mutation on chromosome 4. The mutation is a 'stutter' of between 42 and 100 repeats of the base triplet C–A–G. The number of repeats of the sequence is inversely related to the time of onset of the disease. Death of brain cells results in uncontrolled movements (chorea) and loss of mental functions.

■ Down's syndrome is caused by the presence of three chromosomes 21 in an individual (trisomy 21) or by the presence of two chromosomes 21 together with part of another chromosome 21 joined to a different chromosome (translocation). The condition has recognisable facial effects and produces mild to severe mental retardation.

■ Trisomy 21 arises by nondisjunction. It is not inherited. In most cases the extra chromosome 21 has come from the mother, and the chance of this occurring increases with increased maternal age. Down's syndrome caused by translocation is inherited.

■ The risk of having a child with a particular inherited disorder can be assessed by pedigree analysis or by genetic screening. Screening may be done by karyotype analysis or involve a specific gene probe. Screening may be performed on potential carriers of the disorder, before implantation on an embryo produced by IVF, or on a developing fetus in the uterus. Samples from a developing fetus may be obtained by amniocentesis or by chorionic villus sampling.

■ Genetic counselling provides confidential advice for those people undergoing genetic screening.

■ Gene therapy treats genetic disorders by altering a patient's genotype. In somatic cell therapy a 'normal' allele of the gene concerned is added to body cells.

Mother's haplotypes

A1		A2
B5		B7
C1		C2
D1		D3

Father's haplotypes

A3		A9
B8		B12
C3		C4
D7		D9

Offspring's haplotypes

A1		A9
B5		B12
C1		C4
D1		D9

● *Figure 5.18* Inheritance of HLA haplotypes.

■ Genetic fingerprinting (DNA profiling) reveals the differences in variable number tandem repeats (VNTRs) of the DNA of different individuals. Multi-locus probes produce genetic fingerprints with many bands. Single-locus probes are more sensitive and give genetic fingerprints of only two bands. Normally four different probes are used together, resulting in genetic fingerprints with eight bands.

■ The ABO blood group locus, and the four linked loci of the major histocompatibility complex (MHC)/human leucocyte antigen system (HLA) are important in tissue compatibility in transplant surgery. Incompatible tissue is rejected, so donor and recipient should have the same blood group, and be as closely matched as possible in their HLA system antigens.

■ Each HLA locus has a large number of alleles and so the number of possible genotypes is very large. Since the HLA loci are inherited as a linked block, called a haplotype, the chance of finding a 'match' within a recipient's family is far greater than in the general population.

Questions

1 a Describe the hereditary conditions of cystic fibrosis and Huntington's disease, with particular reference to their genetic transmission.
  b Discuss the social and ethical problems that may arise when genetic abnormalities are detected.

2 a Describe Down's syndrome and explain how it is inherited.
  b Describe how genetic screening for Down's syndrome could be carried out.

3 a Describe how genetic screening is carried out.
  b Discuss the advantages and disadvantages of genetic screening.

4 a Explain the theoretical basis of gene therapy.
  b Discuss the possible benefits and hazards of gene therapy.

5 a Explain the theoretical basis of genetic fingerprinting.
  b Describe the procedures involved in making a genetic fingerprint.

6 a Explain what is meant by **tissue compatibility**.
  b Discuss the significance of tissue compatibility in seeking a suitable donor in transplant surgery.

Answers to self-assessment questions

Chapter 1

1.1 *Parent's genotypes* $Rw^R Rw^S$ $Rw^R Rw^S$

Gametes Rw^R or Rw^S Rw^R or Rw^S

Gametes from one parent

	Rw^R	Rw^S
Rw^R	$Rw^R Rw^R$ resistant high vit. K requirement	$Rw^R Rw^S$ resistant slightly increased vit. K requirement
Rw^S	$Rw^R Rw^S$ resistant slightly increased vit. K requirement	$Rw^S Rw^S$ susceptible normal vit. K requirement

Gametes from the other parent

1.2 **a** Variance (V_P) of Black Mexican parents = $3.57\,cm^2$
V_P of Tom Thumb parents = $0.67\,cm^2$
V_P of offspring 1 = $2.25\,cm^2$

b V_E = the average of the V_P of the parents and offspring 1
= $2.16\,cm^2$

c V_P of offspring 2 = $5.06\,cm^2$
$V_G = V_P - V_E$
= $5.06 - 2.16\,cm^2$
= $2.90\,cm^2$

1.3 **iiCC** and **iiCc**

1.4 *Parent's phenotypes*   pink   white

Parent's genotypes   AAbb   aaBB

Gametes   Ab   aB

F_1 genotypes   AaBb

F_1 phenotypes   purple

Although a pure-breeding white-flowered variety could be either **aaBB** or **aabb**, the latter could not give purple flowers in the F_1 and so is the incorrect choice in this case.

$F_1 \times F_1$ AaBb   AaBb

Gametes   (AB) or (Ab) or (aB) or (ab)   (AB) or (Ab) or (aB) or (ab)

Gametes from one parent

	(AB)	(Ab)	(aB)	(ab)
(AB)	AABB purple	AABb purple	AaBB purple	AaBb purple
(Ab)	AABb purple	AAbb pink	AaBb purple	Aabb pink
(aB)	AaBB purple	AaBb purple	aaBB white	aaBb white
(ab)	AaBb purple	Aabb pink	aaBb white	aabb white

Gametes from the other parent (left label)

F₂ phenotypes

1.5

Parent's phenotypes	white	white
Parent's genotypes	AAbb	aaBB
Gametes	(Ab)	(aB)
F₁ genotypes	AaBb	
F₁ phenotypes	purple	
F₁ × F₁	AaBb	AaBb

Gametes   (AB) or (Ab) or (aB) or (ab)   (AB) or (Ab) or (aB) or (ab)

Gametes from one parent

	(AB)	(Ab)	(aB)	(ab)
(AB)	AABB purple	AABb purple	AaBB purple	AaBb purple
(Ab)	AABb purple	AAbb white	AaBb purple	Aabb white
(aB)	AaBB purple	AaBb purple	aaBB white	aaBb white
(ab)	AaBb purple	Aabb white	aaBb white	aabb white

Gametes from the other parent (left label)

F₂ phenotypes

1.6 **a** 1:1:1:1

b Linkage; that is the two loci are on the same chromosome. The alleles for grey body and straight wings are on one homologous chromosome in the heterozygote, and the alleles for ebony body and curled wings are on the other homologous chromosome.

c $\dfrac{30 + 29}{113 + 30 + 29 + 115} \times 100\% = 20.6\%$

d The curled wing locus is further away from the ebony locus (cross over value = 21%) than is the aristopedia locus (cross over value = 12%).

1.7 **a** The expected ratio of phenotypes expected from a dihybrid test cross is 1:1:1:1. The total number of flies = 180.

Phenotypes of flies	red eyes, normal bristles	red eyes, spineless bristles	claret eyes, normal bristles	claret eyes, spineless bristles
Observed number (O)	53	34	37	56
Expected ratio	1 :	1 :	1 :	1
Expected number (E)	45	45	45	45
O − E	+8	−11	−8	+11
(O − E)²	64	121	64	121
(O − E)²/E	1.42	2.69	1.42	2.69

$\Sigma(O - E)^2/E = 8.22$
$\chi^2 = 8.22$

From *table 1.3*, with degrees of freedom = 3, this value of χ^2 lies between a probability of 0.05 and 0.01. The results are just significantly different from expectation.

b The expected 1:1:1:1 ratio assumed independent assortment. This assumption is not upheld. The two loci are linked.

Chapter 2

2.1 Different species may have different alleles of background genes, so that a hybrid of a particular cross may inherit appropriate alleles from only one parent. Repeated backcrossing to the parental species with appropriate alleles will be necessary.

In an extreme case, parents chosen for their possession of a particular character may both have inappropriate alleles of background genes for the country in which the crop is to be grown. Once the cross is made, the offspring will have to be crossed with a variety with appropriate alleles. Again, repeated backcrossing to that variety will be necessary.

2.2 'New variety 1' is homozygous whereas 'new variety 4' is a mixture of 3 different homozygous lines and therefore has more genetic variation.

Advantage: 'new variety 4' is more likely to be able to adapt to changed conditions (in climate or disease or pests).
Disadvantage: 'new variety 4' may show some variation (in growth or yield or size).

2.3 The parental lines must be isolated to prevent cross-pollination.

The seed parent must be emasculated to prevent self-pollination, and the flowers isolated in bags to prevent cross-pollination from unknown sources.

When pollen has been transferred by hand from the pollen parent, the seed parent flowers must be bagged again to prevent unknown cross-pollination.

Chapter 3

3.1 Hybrids do not 'breed true' if reproduced by seeds, even if self-pollinated. They are heterozygous at various (possibly many) loci and the offspring will show genetic variation. Vegetative reproduction and tissue culture allow the production of a clone of genetically identical offspring (except for any mutations).

3.2 Symbols:

R^{24} = dominant allele giving resistance to race 24 of rust

r^{24} = recessive allele giving susceptibility to race 24 of rust

R^{22} = dominant allele giving resistance to race 22 of rust

r^{22} = recessive allele giving susceptibility to race 22 of rust.

Ottawa genotype: $R^{24}R^{24}r^{22}r^{22}$
Bombay genotype: $r^{24}r^{24}R^{22}R^{22}$

Both varieties are pure breeding and so are homozygous at both loci. The F_1 from these parents would be heterozygous at both loci and resistant to both races of rust.

3.3 In resistant sheep, the incubation period of the disease is longer than the animals' life span. They may carry the agent of the disease; they simply do not show any effects.

3.4 When the patient starts on a course of anti-biotic, only the most susceptible bacteria will be killed. As more antibiotic is taken, bacteria which are less susceptible will be killed. Hence, if a patient starts to take antibiotic, but then stops taking it, the antibiotic has acted as a selective agent favouring bacteria with some degree of resistance.

3.5 a 10 possible genotypes; effectively continuous variation.

b

Genotype	Relative level of resistance
Rop-1^A Rop-1^B	(4.5 + 2.4) = 6.9
Rop-1^B Rop-1^C	(2.4 + 3.85) = 6.25
Rop-1^A Rop-1^C	(4.5 + 3.85) = 8.35

Remember that the effect of the resistance alleles is additive. The relative resistance level of each homozygote shown in *table 3.1* is the result of two alleles.

3.6 a Spraying the cotton crop increases the concentration of insecticide in the general environment. The insecticide acts as a selective agent, killing susceptible *Anopheles*. Some insects are, by chance mutation, resistant. These survive, breed and pass on their resistance to their offspring, increasing the resistance level in the population.

b The level of resistance of the population of *Anopheles* is higher at the start of the spraying period in 1971 than it was in 1970. The same selection for resistance therefore results in a higher level of resistance in the population after the second spraying period.

c When there is no insecticide acting as a selective agent, resistant *Anopheles* must be at some disadvantage in comparison with susceptible insects.

Chapter 4

4.1 Target site is: $- - - - - -$G*C C T G G C$- - - - - -$

$- - - - - -$C G G A C C*G$- - - - - -$

Sticky ends are: $- - - - - -$G   C C T G G C$- - - - - -$

$- - - - - -$C G G A C C   G$- - - - - -$

4.2 Plasmid pBR322 carries genes for ampicillin resistance and tetracycline resistance. Those bacteria taking up unmodified plasmid show both.

In the recombinant plasmid, the inserted gene is put within the gene for tetracycline resistance, inactivating it. The gene for ampicillin resistance is untouched.

Bacteria with no pBR322 are susceptible to both antibiotics.

4.3 **a** The herbicide-resistant tobacco can be sprayed with bromoxynil to reduce competition from weeds. This may increase yield or reduce labour costs.

b The tobacco may now contain bromoxynil which could increase the health risk to smokers. Tests should be carried out to measure the bromoxynil content of the tobacco and to assess the health risks. (This could involve the use of animals.) The presence of the gene for bromoxynil resistance may affect the expression of other genes in the tobacco plant, so the tobacco should be tested for the presence of other 'new' and possibly harmful substances.

4.4 **a** This ensures that the gene is switched on and expressed only in the mammary glands, since the milk protein is produced only there.

b A gene inserted into a fertilised egg, if successfully taken up, is present in all tissues, including the gonads. It can therefore be passed on to offspring.

c DNA analysis from a blood sample, using a gene probe to identify the gene.

4.5 The potential risk is greatest with bacteria, because genes may be passed from modified bacteria by horizontal transmission into other bacteria. Such transfers could have unforeseen effects.

4.6 Virus treatment reduces caterpillar damage compared with the untreated control plants. Plants treated with genetically modified viruses showed less damage than those treated with unmodified viruses. Treatment with viruses at the higher dose rate reduces leaf damage.

In comparison with the control plants, damage is reduced by low doses of unmodified virus to 93%, and genetically modified virus to 65%. Damage is reduced by high doses of unmodified virus to 59%, and of genetically modified virus to 46%.

Chapter 5

5.1 **a** (Autosomal) dominant. All sufferers have an affected parent. The number of sufferers and non-sufferers in the offspring is approximately 1:1. The same pattern could be obtained if the mutation were recessive, but this would require two marriages, one in the first, and one in the second generation, between a homozygote recessive and a heterozygote. This is unlikely given that the disorder is rare.

b 1 in 2 / $\frac{1}{2}$ / 0.5

5.2 When a genetic disorder is the result of a recessive allele of a gene, the 'normal' allele is dominant. The introduced dominant allele will effectively convert the individual to being a heterozygote for the gene, producing some correct product of the gene. The recessive allele may code for a defective product or not be successfully transcribed. In either case, production of some correct product should cure the disorder.

5.3 Four bands in the child's profile match four of the bands in the mother's. The other four bands in the child's profile match four bands of the possible father's profile. The possible father *is* the father.

5.4 **a** **i** Red cells from group O have no red cell antigens. They cannot be clumped by the recipient's plasma antibodies.

ii AB blood has no plasma antibodies and will not clump the donor red cells.

In both of these cases the volume donated is small. This means that the donated plasma antibodies can be ignored, because the small volume is rapidly mixed with the recipient's blood.

b If large volumes are to be donated, the effect of the donated plasma antibodies on the recipient's red cells must be considered. The recipient's cells would be clumped.

5.5 **a** 1 in 4 / $\frac{1}{4}$ / 0.25

b 1 in 4 / $\frac{1}{4}$ / 0.25